W. Warren Bentley

Great Joy! A New and Favorite Collection of Hymns and Music

for gospel meetings, prayer, temperance, and camp meetings, and for Sunday schools

W. Warren Bentley

Great Joy! A New and Favorite Collection of Hymns and Music
for gospel meetings, prayer, temperance, and camp meetings, and for Sunday schools

ISBN/EAN: 9783337089412

Printed in Europe, USA, Canada, Australia, Japan

Cover: Foto ©Lupo / pixelio.de

More available books at **www.hansebooks.com**

GREAT JOY!

A NEW AND FAVORITE COLLECTION
OF HYMNS AND MUSIC,

→ FOR ←

GOSPEL MEETINGS,

PRAYER, TEMPERANCE, AND
CAMP MEETINGS,

AND

SUNDAY SCHOOLS,

— BY —

WILLIAM W. BENTLEY, ALFRED BEIRLY,
AND
Mrs. M. E. WILLSON.

PUBLISHED BY
GEORGE D. NEWHALL & CO.,
50 West Fourth St., Cincinnati, O.

LIST OF AUTHORS:

W. W. Bentley,
Jno. R. Sweney,
T. C. O'Kane,
J. E. Hall,
J. H. Tenney,
P. P. Bliss,
E. S. Lorentz,
J. W. Bischoff,
Theo. E. Perkins,
W. T. Giffe,
J. E. Rankin,
H. R. Palmer,
W. G. Fischer,
Wm. Johnson,
Geo. C. Hugg,
R. Porter Orr,
H. J. Schonacker,

Alfred Beirly,
Frank M. Davis,
Karl Reden,
W. A. Ogden,
A. J. Abbey,
Sophia C. Hall,
T. J. Shanks,
Chas. H. Gabriel,
D. B. Towner,
Mrs. Jos. F. Knapp,
C. C. Converse,
H. Sanders,
C. C. Case,
Geo. A. Minor,
Miss Dora Boole,
G. P. Benjamin,
Rev. L. Hartsough.
Fannie Crosby.

Mrs. M. E. Wilson,

Copyright, 1881,
by
GEORGE D. NEWHALL.

PREFACE.

We send forth *GREAT JOY!* with a sincere desire that its songs may be instrumental in winning many precious souls. We feel grateful to the Favorite Authors who have enriched our work by their contributions.

W. W. BENTLEY,
ALFRED BEIRLY,
Mrs. M. E. WILLSON.

New York, 1881.

GREETING

BY

FANNY CROSBY,

"GREAT JOY," our newly finished work,
   We dedicate with prayer,
To earnest seekers after God,
   And Christians everywhere.
"GREAT JOY" its name, "GREAT JOY" it sings,
   "GREAT JOY" from every page
Is gushing forth, like crystal springs,
   To comfort youth and age.

We send it broadcast o'er the land,
   To tell the mighty love
Of Christ, our best, and dearest Friend
   In earth, or heaven above.
We, for His glory send it forth
   With this, our hearts' request,
That through its songs, poor, hopeless ones
   May be redeemed and blest.

"GREAT JOY!" O may its voice resound,
   And careless sleepers wake,
Till mingled tones of love and praise,
   From new-born souls shall break.
We hope to see our little work
   Fast spreading, far and wide,
And millions coming home to Him,
   Who once for sinners died.

New York, March 1st., 1881.

No. 2. THE MERCY SEAT.

"For where two or three are gathered."—Matt. 18: 20.

FANNY J. CROSBY.   JNO. R. SWENEY.

1. From worldly thought and busy care, We come to seek the place of prayer,
2. O hallowed hour that nearer brings To mortal view, e-ter-nal things,
3. Come, burdened soul, if such there be, Who from thy sorrow would'st be free;
4. Praise God that all the cross may bear, Praise God that all a crown may wear,

Where Jes-sus con-descends to meet His children at the mer-cy-seat.
While here we hold communion sweet With Je-sus, at the mer-cy-seat.
Thy lov-ing Sav-ior now will meet, And cleanse thee at the mer-cy-seat.
Praise God for such an hour so sweet, Of blessing at the mer-cy-seat.

REFRAIN.

The mer-cy-seat, the mer-cy-seat, Our on-ly safe and sure retreat;

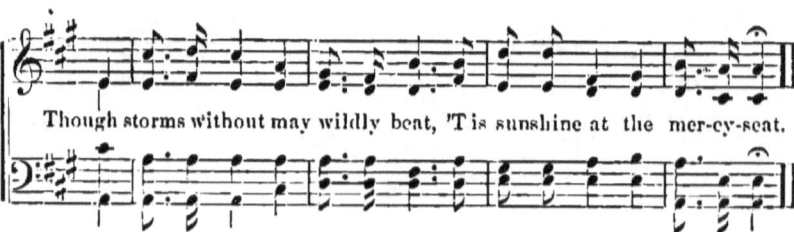

Though storms without may wildly beat, 'Tis sunshine at the mer-cy-seat.

From "Joy to the World," by permission.

ABUNDANTLY ABLE TO SAVE. Concluded.

for sinners he gave,   And he is a-bun - dantly a-ble to save.
a ransom for sinners he gave,   And he is abundantly able to save.

No. 11.   SALVATION FULL AND FREE.

JAMES NICHOLSON.   JNO. R. SWENEY.

1. Sal-va-tion full and free! Was purchased for mankind; The message is to
2. Sal-va-tion full and free! Oh words of blessed cheer; Sinner, it is for

CHORUS.

thee, Tho' lame and halt and blind. Oh! come, Oh! come, Oh! come while yet you
thee,   The glorious message hear.   Oh! come, Oh! come,

may, Sal-va-tion's full and free to all, O sin-ner! come to-day.

3 Salvation full and free!
   Believer, drop thy load;
   For peace and purity,
   Were bought with Jesus' blood.

4 Salvation full and free!
   Salvation from all sin!
   Is offered now to thee;
   By simple faith step in.

No. 12. IS IT THERE? WRITTEN THERE?

"Written in the Lamb's Book of Life."—Rev. 21: 27.

J. E. Rankin, D. D. E. S. Lorenz.

1. I do not ask for the pride of earth, For the pride of wealth or the pride of birth; Be this, the rath-er, my one great care; In the Book of Life, that my name is there.
2. I do not ask for a glorious name, That is written high on the scroll of Fame; Be this, the rath-er, con-cern of mine, To in-sure it there, in that Book divine.
3. I do not ask that my earthly life Should be free from burdens, and cares and strife; Nor that its cur-rent have tranquil flow, If but this one thing I may sure-ly know.
4. I'd give up all that I hope be-low, All that time can give, or the world be-stow; If when the Lord in his king-dom come, He will know me then, and will take me home.

CHORUS.

In the Book of Life, on those pages fair, Do the angels see that my name is there? In the Book of Life, on those pa-ges fair, Is it there? Is it there? written there? written there?

From "Gospel Bells." By per.

No. 13. O PRODIGAL, DON'T STAY AWAY.

"I will arise and go unto my father."—LUKE 15: 18.

J. E. RANKIN, D. D.
J. W. BISCHOFF.

1. O prod-i-gal, don't stay a-way! The Fa-ther is wait-ing to-day, There's room and to spare; There is rai-ment to wear: O
2. O prod-i-gal brother, come home! Why longer in wretchedness roam? You're lone-ly and lost, You are driv-en and tost: O
3. O prod-i-gal, what will you do? Love's table is wait-ing for you; For-give-ness so sweet, Sure, your com-ing will greet: O
4. O prod-i-gal, brother, a-rise! For par-don, look up to the skies; No lon-ger then stray From thy Fa-ther, a-way: O

CHORUS.

prod-igal, don't stay away. Will you come, will you come?
prod-igal brother, come home.
prod-igal, what will you do?
prod-igal, brother, a-rise.
will you come? will you come?

Will you come, come home to-day? will you come? There is welcome for you, There's a kiss, kind and true, Then, O prod-i-gal, don't stay a-way.

From "Gospel Bells." By per.

No. 14. COME AND BE BLEST.

J. E. H.   J. E. HALL.

1. To the Savior's waiting arms, To the sweetness of his charms, From thy fears and dread alarms,
2. To the fountain bright and clear; If a-thirst, do now draw near, Come, says Jesus, do not fear;
3. To the feast so rich and free, Amply spread for you and me, Where our wants supplied may be,
4. In the rock's safe shadow hide; From the storms which now betide, There securely e'er abide;

CHORUS.

Come, come, way-worn, come. Jesus kindly intercedes,
Come, come, traveler, come.
Come, come, dear one, come.
Come, come, lost one, come.

Now for you he loving pleads. Tell him all your wants and needs, Come, be blest, come, find rest.

No. 15. I CHOOSE TO FOLLOW JESUS.

"And they forsook all and followed him."—Luke 5: 7.

JOSEPHINE POLLARD. THEODORE E. PERKINS. By per.

1. I choose to fol-low Je-sus all the way, all the way,
2. I choose to fol-low Je-sus all the way, all the way,
3. I choose to fol-low Je-sus all the way, all the way,
4. I cast my lot with Je-sus, tho' I may, all the way,

He will keep me so I shall not go a-stray, all the way,
For He knoweth what my needs are ev-'ry day; all the way,
For He'll watch ov-er the lambs that go a-stray; all the way,
Find it hard His lov-ing coun-sels to o-bey; all the way,

Tho' I suf-fer pain and loss, In the beaming of the cross,
By a path of liv-ing light, He di-rects me thro' the night,
Tho' they fall in Sa-tan's track, He will bring them safely back,
He is read-y strength to give, By His grace a-lone I live,

Yet I choose to fol-low Je-sus all the way.
So I choose to fol-low Je-sus all the way.
So I choose to fol-low Je-sus all the way.
So I choose to fol-low Je-sus all the way.

From "Coronation Songs."

No. 16. IS THERE ANY ONE HERE?

"Amend your ways and your doings, and I will cause you to dwell in this place."—Jas. 7: 3.

E. R. LATTA. W. T. GIFFE.

1. Is there a-ny one here whose heart is touched, By a pen-i-tent sor-row for sin? Let him come and ob-tain sal-va-tion now, And the work of the Mas-ter be-gin; We have slight-ed his love and grace divine, Yet he wait-eth our sins to for-

2. Is there a-ny one here whose heart is touched, By the sound of the heav-en-ly strain That comes from the an-gels who tell his birth, As the shepherds keep watch on the plain? Let him come and ob-tain sal-va-tion now, To the gra-cious Re-deem-er ap-

3. Is there a-ny one here whose heart is touched By the fin-ger of in-fi-nite love? Let him come and ob-tain sal-va-tion now, Let him start for the cit-y a-bove! We will wan-der no more a-way from thee, At the al-tar of mer-cy we

From "Helping Hand." By per.

18

IS THERE ANY ONE HERE? Concluded.

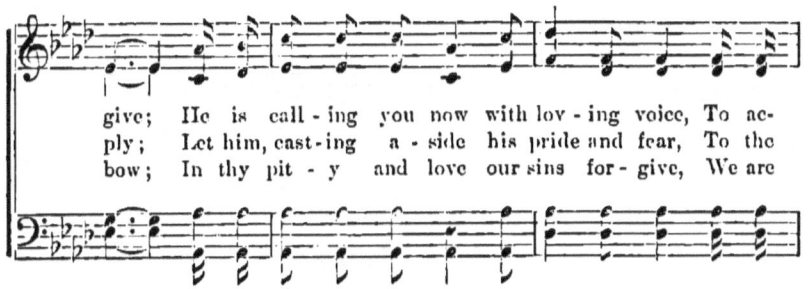

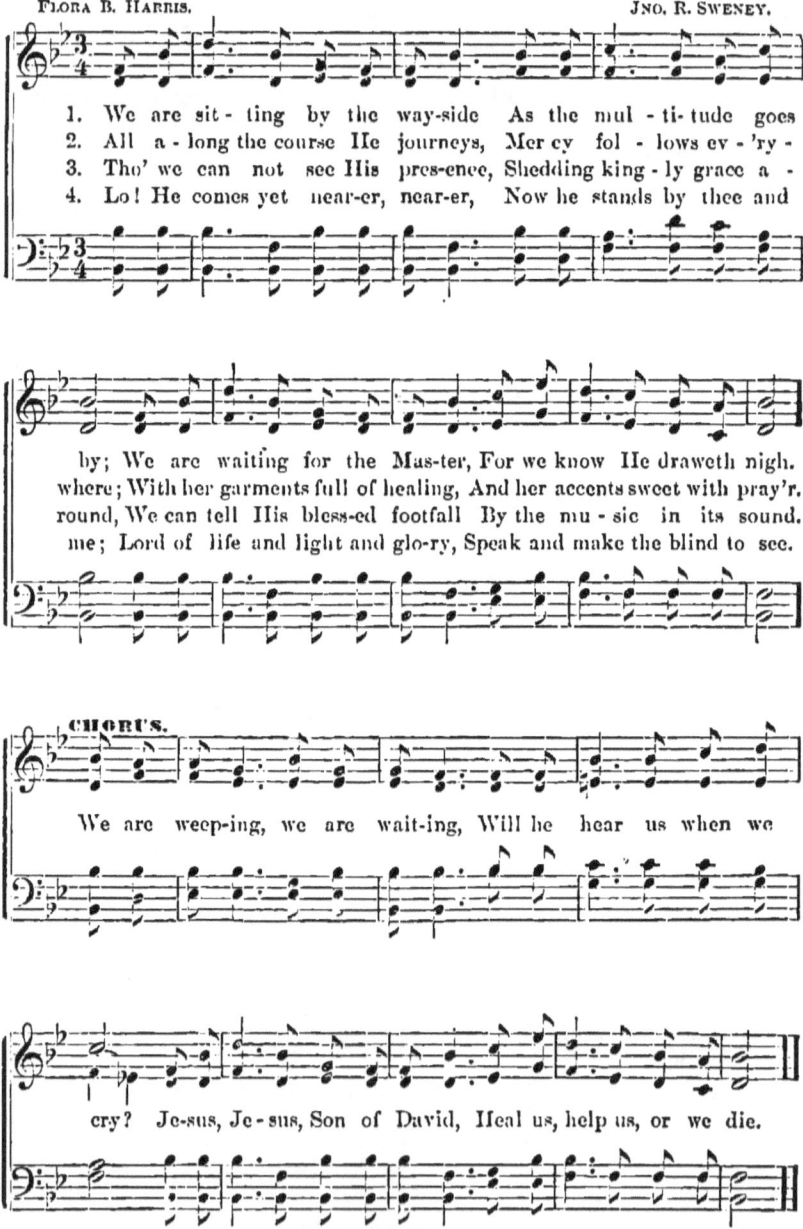

No. 18. WHEN I WALK THRO' THE VALLEY.

"Though I walk through the valley of the shadow of death, I will fear no evil."—Ps. 23: 4.

J. E. RANKIN, D. D.   J. E. RANKIN.

1. When I walk thro' the val-ley of death, When I yield up to Je-sus my breath, No e-vil I'll fear, Since my Mas-ter is near; Can I doubt the kind words that he saith?

2. I will lean my poor head on His breast, I will sleep the sweet sleep of the blest; No troub-le or care Shall op-press my soul there, As He hush-es my spir-it to rest.

3. I will come, come a-gain, if I go, And the place and the way well ye know; A home I pre-pare, In those man-sions so fair, For the lost, who love me here be-low.

REFRAIN.

I will come, I will come, I will come, I will come, I will come and take you home, Oh, be ye not dismayed, Oh, be ye not a-fraid When ye walk through the val-ley of death.

From "Gospel Bells," by per.

No. 19. COME, SINNER, COME.

"Come unto me, all ye that labor and are heavy laden.—Matt. 11:28."

WILL. ELLSWORTH WITTER.   H. R. PALMER.

1. While Je-sus whis-pers to you, Come, sin-ner, come!
2. Are you too heav-y lad-en? Come, sin-ner, come!
3. Oh, hear His ten-der plead-ing, Come, sin-ner, come!

While we are pray-ing for you, Come, sin-ner, come!
Je-sus will bear your bur-den, Come, sin-ner, come!
Come, and re-ceive the bless-ing, Come, sin-ner, come!

Now is the time to own Him, Come, sin-ner, come!
Je-sus will not de-ceive you, Come, sin-ner, come!
While Je-sus whis-pers to you, Come, sin-ner, come!

Now is the time to know Him, Come, sin-ner, come!
Je-sus can now re-deem you, Come, sin-ner, come!
While we are pray-ing for you, Come, sin-ner, come!

By permission.

IS YOUR LAMP BURNING, BROTHER? Concluded.

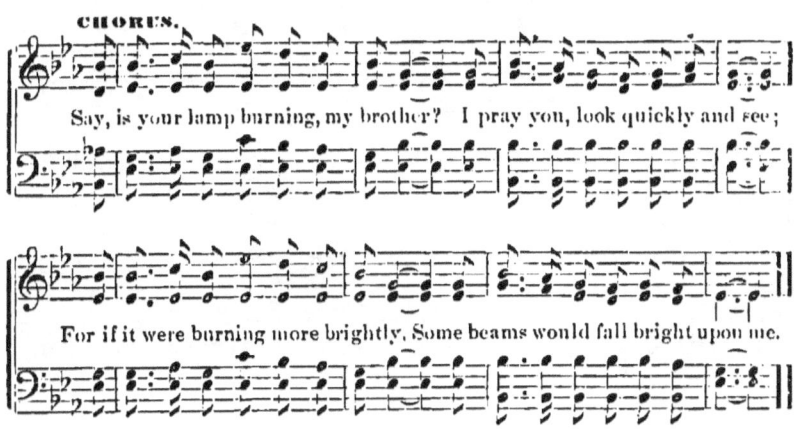

Say, is your lamp burning, my brother? I pray you, look quickly and see;
For if it were burning more brightly, Some beams would fall bright upon me.

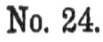

LEAD ME ON.

KARL REDEN.

1. Trav'ling to the bet-ter land, O'er the de-sert's scorching sand,

Father! let me grasp thy hand; Lead me on, lead me on!

2 When at Marah, parched with heat,
 I the sparkling fountain greet,
 Make the bitter waters sweet;
  Lead me on!

3 When the wilderness is drear,
 Show me Elim's palm-groves near,
 And her wells as crystal clear;
  Lead me on!

4 Through the water, thro' the fire,
 Never let me fall or tire,
 Every step brings Canaan nigher:
  Lead me on!
 By permission.

5 Bid me stand on Nebo's height,
 Gaze upon the land of light,
 Then transported with the sight,
  Lead me on!

6 When I stand on Jordan's brink,
 Never let me fear or shrink;
 Hold me, Father, lest I sink;
  Lead me on!

7 When the victory is won,
 And my earthly work is done,
 Up to glory lead me on!
  Lead me on! lead me on!

No. 27. TRUSTING IN THE PROMISE.

"He is faithful that promised."—HEB. x: 23.

Rev. H. B. HARTZLER. E. S. LORENZ.

1. I have found repose for my wea-ry soul, Trusting in the promise of the
2. I will sing my song as the day goes by, Trusting in the promise of the
3. Oh, the peace and joy of the life I live, Trusting in the promise of the

Sav-ior; And a har-bor safe when the bil-lows roll,
Sav-ior; And re-joice in hope, while I live or die,
Sav-ior; Oh, the strength and grace on-ly God can give,

Trusting in the promise of the Sav-ior, I will fear no foe
Trusting in the promise of the Sav-ior, I can smile at grief,
Trusting in the promise of the Sav-ior, Who-so-ev-er will

in the dead-ly strife, Trusting in the prom-ise of the
and a-bide in pain, Trusting in the prom-ise of the
may be saved to-day, Trusting in the prom-ise of the

By permission.

TRUSTING IN THE PROMISE, Concluded,

31

No. 28. FOR OTHER FOUNDATION.

"For other foundation can no man lay than that is laid, which is Jesus Christ."—1 Cor. 3: 11.

PAULINA. ALFRED BEIRLY.

1. O Build-ers, haste to the Rock a-way, For Je-sus Christ is the cor-ner stone; We sing His praise as we build to-day, "For oth-er foun-da-tion can no man lay."
2. We builded long on the sands of sin; Our wrecks went out as the tide came in; By snares of Sa-tan no more en-ticed, We build a-lone on the Rock of Christ.
3. The rains descend and the tempests rave, But trust-ing One who a-lone can save, We sing His praise, and we'll sing for aye, That "oth-er foun-da-tions can no man lay."

REFRAIN.

O Builders, haste to the Rock a-way, "For oth-er foun-da-tion can no man lay, For oth-er foun-da-tion can no man lay."

By permission.

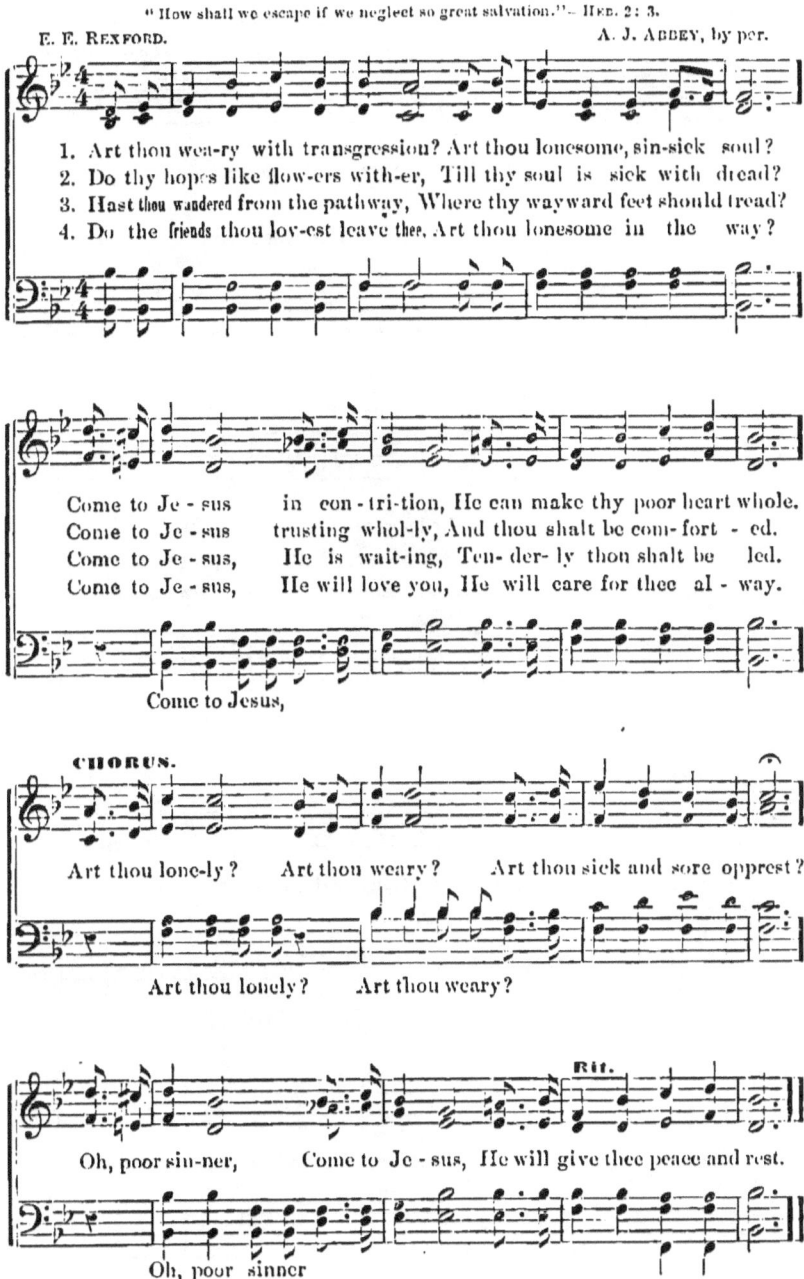

No. 30. HAIL THE GREAT EMANCIPATION.

"Fear not: for, behold, I bring you good tidings of great joy, which shall be to all people."— Luke 2: 10.

ALFRED BEIRLY.

1. God, th'all-wise, beholding sinners, Said, "my people I'll re-claim;"
2. One great sac-ri-fice was need-ed, One a-tonement for us all;
3. High o'er all the worlds in glo-ry, With the Father now is He;

From His throne the world's Redeem-er On that ho-ly mission came.
Christ, the liv-ing Son of prom-ise, Died God's people to re-call.
Round the throne celes-tial ar-mies Sing Him praise eter-nal-ly.

CHORUS.

Hail, the great E-man-ci-pa-tion! Millions of earth-bondsmen freed,
Come from ev-'ry clime and station, Who for freedom learn their need.

By permission.

No. 31. ONCE FOR ALL.

Rev. J. H. Martin, D. D.
T. C. O'Kane.
Written for this work.

1. Once for all the Sav-ior died, Christ the Lord was cru-ci-fied; Once for all He shed His blood, Pouring forth a crim-son flood.
2. Once for all our sins He bore, Bought our peace for-ev-er-more; Once for all our debt He paid, Full, complete a-tone-ment made.
3. Once for all the Sav-ior rose, Vic-tor o'er His might-y foes, With their glorious king and head, Saints shall waken from the dead.
4. Once for all as-cend-ing high, Throned and crowned above the sky, There He in-ter-cedes and reigns, Praise Him in triumphant strains.

CHORUS.

Oh be-lieve Him and be blest, Oh receive Him and find rest; All your sins shall be for-giv'n, You shall reign with him in heav'n.

By permission.

No. 32. **GLIDING DOWN LIFE'S RIVER.**

"I must work the works of Him that sent me, while it is day."—John 9: 4.

J. E. R. J. E. Rankin, D. D.

1. In this world of sin and ru-in, Glid-ing down Life's river,
2. We must lift the Cross a-bove us! Glid-ing down Life's river:
3. We must raise our fall-en broth-er, Glid-ing down Life's river:

There is work we must be do-ing, Gliding down Life's river: Ev-'ry
We must work for those who love us, Gliding down Life's river: We must
We must help and cheer each other; Gliding down Life's river: Where the

day there's something new, Which the Lord would have us do, Work for
ear-ly toil and late; Must o-bey and not de-bate; We must
weak or tempted stand, We must heed our Lord's command: We must

me, and work for you, Gliding down Life's river, Gliding down Life's river.
pray, and we must wait, Gliding down Life's river, Gliding down Life's river.
lend a helping hand, Gliding down Life's river, Gliding down Life's river.

4 We must never faint nor falter,
Gliding down Life's river:
What if come, or cross, or halter,
Gliding down Life's river?
Let the world make its ado,
To our Lord we must be true;
Must be Christian through and through,
Gliding down Life's river.

5 We must soothe the sick and sighing,
Gliding down Life's river!
We must point to Christ the dying,
Gliding down Life's river!
We must keep the goal in view:
Must our Master's steps pursue;
We must do, what he would do,
Gliding down Life's river.

From "Gospel Bells." By per.

No. 33. HE'LL RECEIVE YOU.

"Him that cometh to me I will in no wise cast out."—John 6: 37.

A. J. Abbey.

Moderato.

1. Come, poor sinner, come to Je - sus, Now His pre-cious call o - bey;
2. Has - ten to Him, while He's calling, He is wait - ing, waiting still;
3. Time is fly - ing, swiftly fly - ing, Earthly scenes will soon be o'er;
4. Sin - ner, has-ten to the Sav - ior, In your youthful days, and best,

He'll re - ceive you, He will par - don, Oh, ac - cept Him while 'tis day.
List - en to His ear - nest plead-ing; Ev - 'ry prom-ise He'll ful - fill.
Sav - ior grant Thy pard'ning bless-ing, Save us on the "golden shore."
Give to Him your heart and serv - ice, And re-ceive e - ter - nal rest.

REFRAIN. Cres.

Je - sus loves you, ev - er loves you, Gave His life your soul to save;

Rit.

Come in sor - row and con - tri - tion, He'll re-ceive you, and for - give.

By permission.

JESUS IS PASSING THIS WAY. Concluded.

While He is near, oh, believe Him, O-pen your heart to receive Him, For Je-sus is pass-ing this way, ... Is pass-ing this way to-day.
this way,

No. 37.   I AM THINE.

"Lo, we have left all, and have followed Thee."—MARK 10: 28.

ANON.   P.

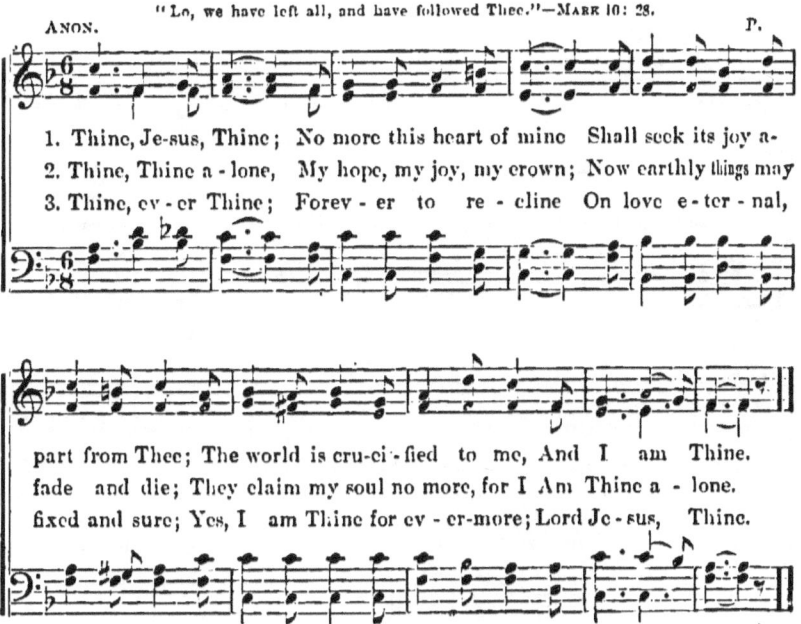

1. Thine, Je-sus, Thine; No more this heart of mine Shall seek its joy a-part from Thee; The world is cru-ci-fied to me, And I am Thine.
2. Thine, Thine a-lone, My hope, my joy, my crown; Now earthly things may fade and die; They claim my soul no more, for I Am Thine a-lone.
3. Thine, ev-er Thine; Forev-er to re-cline On love e-ter-nal, fixed and sure; Yes, I am Thine for ev-er-more; Lord Je-sus, Thine.

No. 39. **WILT THOU RECEIVE ME?**

"But when he was yet a great way off his father saw him."—Luke 15: 20.

W. W. SMITH.   FRANK M. DAVIS.

1. Far from my Fa - ther, Sad, lone and poor I roam,
2. Self, all I give Thee, Naught that I have with-hold;
3. Praise be to Je - sus; Praise Him, ye hosts on high;

Wilt thou re - ceive me home, Fa - ther di - vine?
To thine own im - age mold, Oh make me clean.
Safe in His arms I lie, Safe, safe a - gain.

How can I long - er stray, Starv - ing from day to day?
I bring but bit - ter need, Sins for which Thou didst bleed,
Safe from the tempter's dart, Safe in thy lov - ing heart,

No more will I de - lay, Homeward I turn.
I but thy prom - ise plead, Je - sus, my Lord.
Ne'er may I more de - part, Sav - ior, from Thee.

By permission.

43

WATCHMAN! TELL US. Concluded.

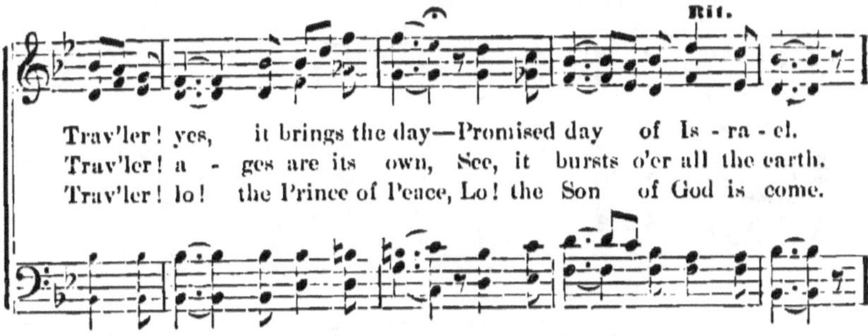

Trav'ler! yes, it brings the day—Promised day of Is-ra-el.
Trav'ler! a-ges are its own, See, it bursts o'er all the earth.
Trav'ler! lo! the Prince of Peace, Lo! the Son of God is come.

No. 44.   MORE LOVE TO THEE.

MRS. E. PRENTISS. "Who loved me, and gave Himself for me."—GAL. 2: 20.   A. BEIRLY.

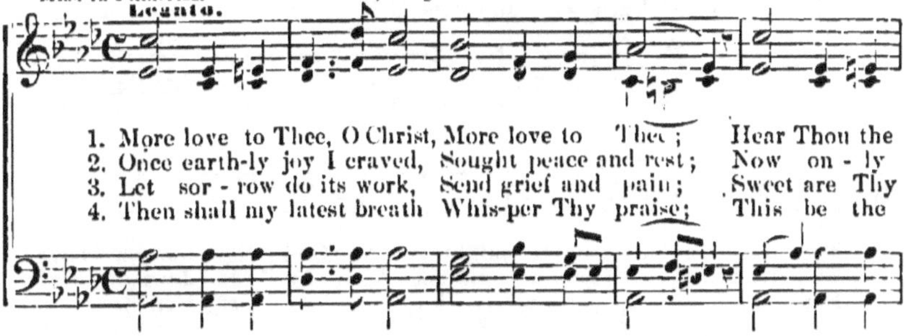

Legato.

1. More love to Thee, O Christ, More love to Thee; Hear Thou the
2. Once earth-ly joy I craved, Sought peace and rest; Now on-ly
3. Let sor-row do its work, Send grief and pain; Sweet are Thy
4. Then shall my latest breath Whis-per Thy praise; This be the

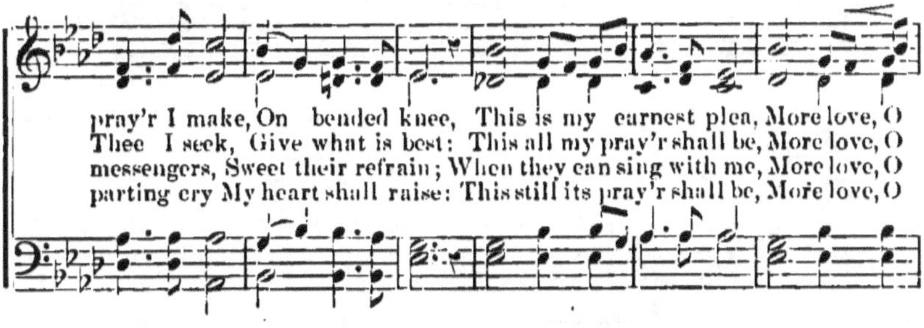

pray'r I make, On bended knee, This is my earnest plea, More love, O
Thee I seek, Give what is best: This all my pray'r shall be, More love, O
messengers, Sweet their refrain; When they can sing with me, More love, O
parting cry My heart shall raise: This still its pray'r shall be, More love, O

Christ, to Thee, More love, O Christ, to Thee, More love to Thee.
Christ, to Thee, More love, O Christ, to Thee, More love to Thee.
Christ, to Thee, More love, O Christ, to Thee, More love to Thee.
Christ, to Thee, More love, O Christ, to Thee, More love to Thee.

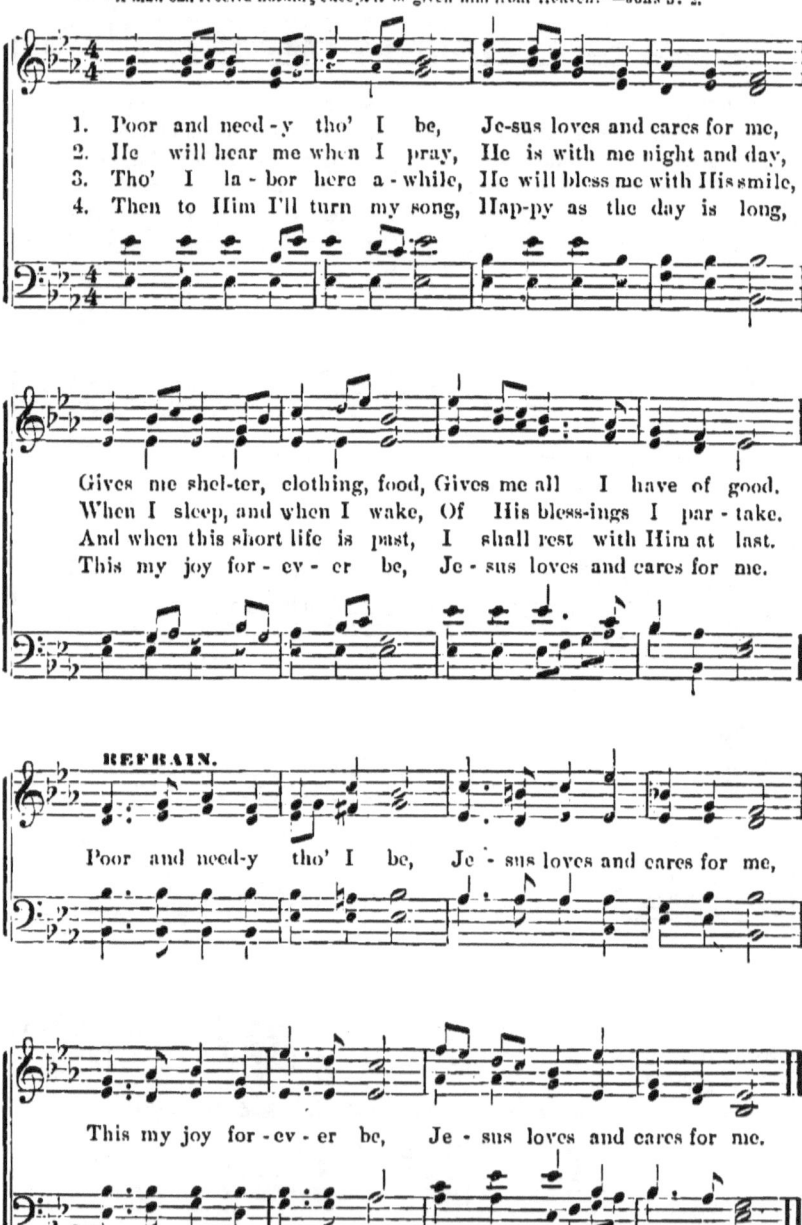

No. 49. BETHESDA IS OPEN FOR THEE.

"Wilt thou be made whole?"—John 5: 6.

Rev. F. Denison. W. Warren Bentley.

1. Bethesda is open, the angel has come, The Spirit is calling for thee;
2. Come, press to the waters while mercy is here, Accept of a cleansing complete;
3. The house of Bethesda for sinners was built, The pool is a fountain of love;
4. Then come to the Fountain, ye needy and lost, Come now while the Savior is nigh;

The waters are troubled, behold there is room, Salvation thro' Jesus is free.
Oh, hear the entreaty dismissing your fear, Lo! judgment and mercy now meet.
The waters are troubled for canceling guilt; And still for our healing now move.
This grace has been purchased at infinite cost, And they that reject it must die.

CHORUS.

Sal-va-tion is free, sal-va-tion is free, Salvation thro' Je-sus is free;

The waters are troubled, behold there is room, Bethesda is open for thee.

By permission.

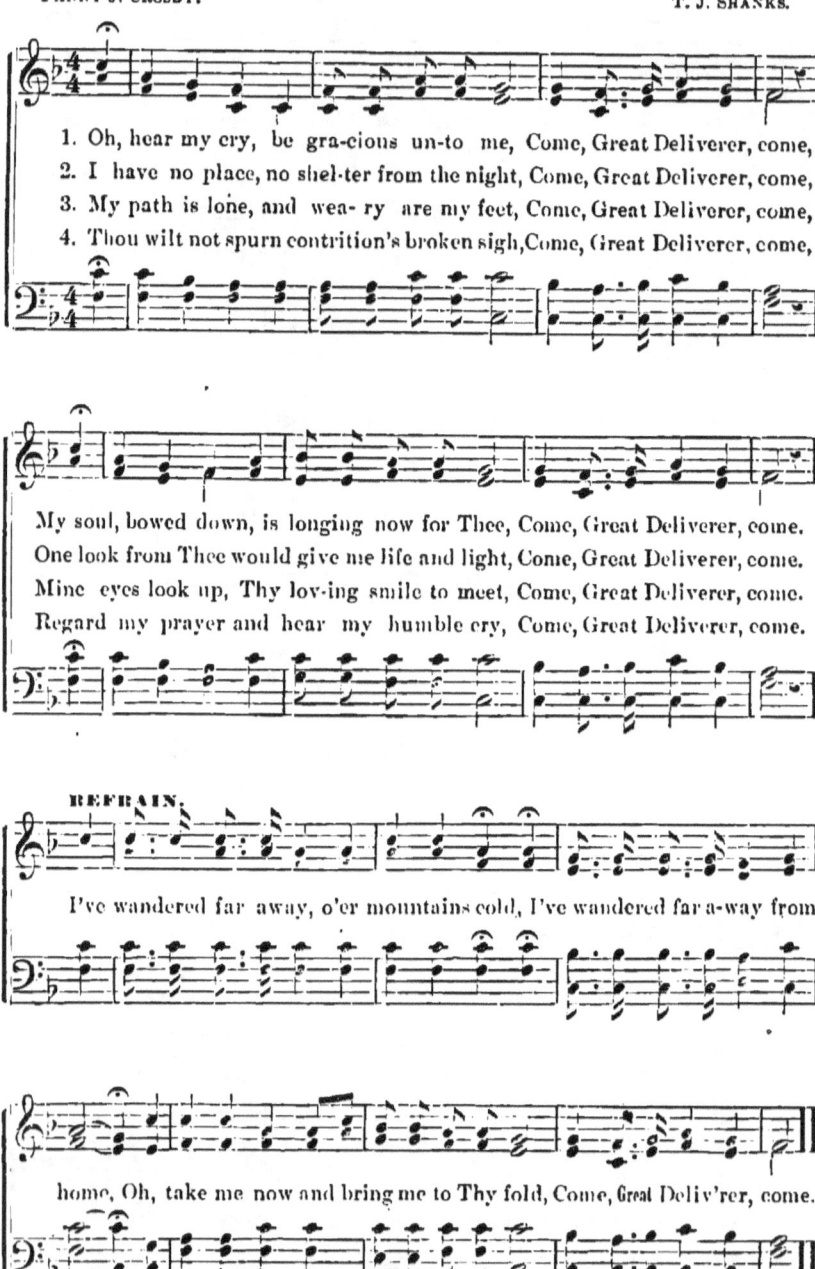

No. 53. REDEEMED.

"My lips shall greatly rejoice when I sing unto Thee, and my soul, which Thou hast redeemed."—
PSALM 71: 23.

ALFRED BEIRLY. ALFRED BEIRLY.

1. "Redeemed!" oh, wondrous love divine, Bestowed on all that do believe;
2. "Redeemed!" we seek no path unknown To One himself the only way;
3. "Redeemed!" our hopes are fixed alone On heav'n and happiness secure;
4. "Redeemed!" then but a few more tears, And we from pain shall ever rest;

Our Father's mercies brightly shine O'er all who will His Christ receive.
But fol-low in His footsteps shown, That lead us on to end-less day.
With Him who did for all a-tone, Of sin no more we need en-dure.
Receive us, Thou, who quells our fears, To live forev-er with the blest.

CHORUS.

In yonder home, around the throne, We'll meet, no more to sever,

In yonder home, around the throne,

There we shall raise glad songs of praise To Christ, our King, forever.

By permission of J. CHURCH & Co.

JESUS, ALL THE WAY. Concluded.

CHORUS.

'Tis Je - sus in the morn-ing hours, And Je - sus thro' the day, And Je - sus in life's ev - en - time, And Je - sus all the way.

No. 56.   **ONLY BELIEVE.**

"Be not afraid, only believe."—MARK 5: 36.

REV. S. D. PHELPS, D. D.   WILLIAM W. BENTLEY.

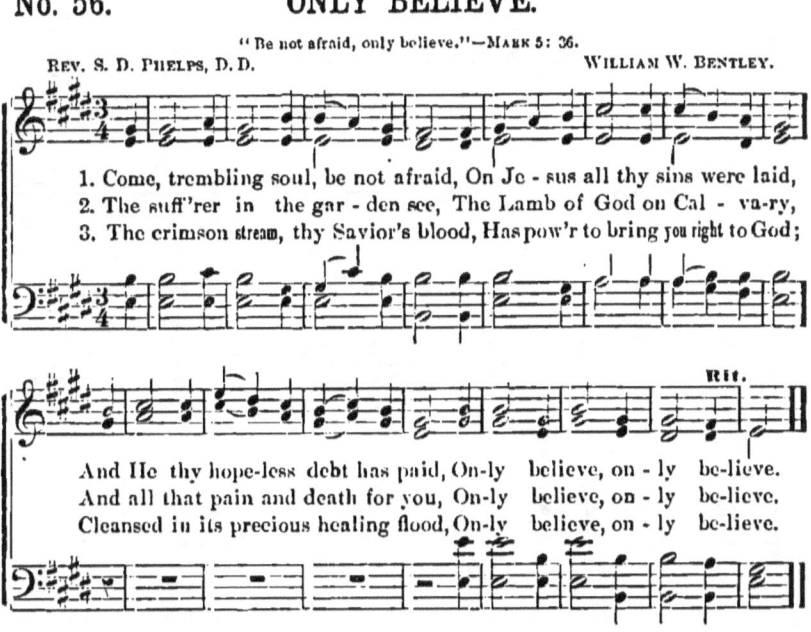

1. Come, trembling soul, be not afraid, On Je - sus all thy sins were laid,
2. The suff'rer in the gar - den see, The Lamb of God on Cal - va - ry,
3. The crimson stream, thy Savior's blood, Has pow'r to bring you right to God;

And He thy hope-less debt has paid, On-ly believe, on - ly be-lieve.
And all that pain and death for you, On-ly believe, on - ly be-lieve.
Cleansed in its precious healing flood, On-ly believe, on - ly be-lieve.

4 In wondrous love he calls to-day,
Cast now thy guilty doubts away,
Free pardon take without delay,
Only believe, only believe.

5 For Thee, O Christ, all things I leave,
To Thee, my Savior, now I cleave.
And I, as Thou dost me receive,
Only believe, only believe.

No. 60. SING AND REJOICE.

"Rejoice and be exceeding glad: for great is your reward in heaven."—MATT. 5: 12.

Rev. I Baltzell.

Spirited.

1. Ye val-iant soldiers of the cross, Ye hap-py pil-grim band,
2. Your Jesus once, "without the camp," Bought liberty for you;
3. Our bugle ne'er shall sound re-treat, While Je-sus leads us on;
4. Your weary feet shall walk the street All paved with gold, on high:

Tho' in this world you suf-fer loss, Press on to Canaan's land.
Then bravely fight for truth and right, And keep your crown in view.
We will not lay our weapons by Un-til we wear the crown.
And He who wore a crown of thorns, Will crown you in the sky.

REFRAIN.

Re - joice, . . . re - joice, . . .
Oh, sing and rejoice, oh, sing and rejoice, We'll soon have a crown to wear;

Re - joice, . . . re - joice, . . . We'll soon . . . . be there.
Oh, sing and rejoice, oh, sing and rejoice, We'll soon, we'll soon be there.

No. 62. **WILT THOU BLESS ME?**

"Blessed are the poor in spirit: for their's is the kingdom of heaven."—MATT. 5: 3.

ALFRED BEIRLY.

1. Oh, my Father, wilt Thou bless me, For my heart is sore dis-trest;
2. Wilt Thou, in the darkness leaning, Gently touch my outstretched hand?

I have wandered sad and lonely, And I long for rest, sweet rest;
Send a ray of light to guide me To the beauteous fa-ther-land!

There is naught on earth to comfort One so weak and wea-ry grown:
And from out the val-ley lead me, When the night is drear and long;

Naught that shall prove strong and steadfast, And I can not walk a-lone.
Teach me how to love and praise Thee With a new and gladsome song.

WILT THOU BLESS ME? Concluded.

REFRAIN.

Oh, my Father, wilt Thou bless me, For my heart is sore distrest;
I have wandered sad and lonely, And I long for rest, sweet rest.

No. 63. JESUS, MY SAVIOR DEAR. 6s & 4s.

E. R. LATTA.   WILLIAM W. BENTLEY.

1. Jesus, my Savior dear, Thy loving voice I hear Inviting me,
2. Thou hast entreated long, To woo my soul from wrong, My sins to blot,
3. How couldst Thou suffer so, To save my soul from woe, To make me Thine;

And from my wanderings, Mid earth's embittered springs, Just now, dear
And now my willing heart Would fain from sin depart; I come, re-
Help me, blest Lamb, I pray, To cast my doubts away, To cast my

Lord, I come, I come to Thee.
fuse me not, I come to Thee.
doubts away, And call Thee mine.

4 Oh, listen to my cry,
Thy precious blood apply,
I now implore;
My heart, blest Savior, take,
And there Thy dwelling make,
And there Thy dwelling make,
For evermore.

TAKE THOU MY HAND. Concluded.

du - ty, Lord, how sin-ful slow; What is my life with-
strong and lov-est me, I know; Lead me, my Lord, to

out re-proving care! Take Thou my hand, and guide me as I go.
see Thy blessed face, Hold fast my hand, and guide me as I go.

No. 67.   OUR COMFORTER AND GUIDE.

"I will not leave you comfortless."—John 14: 18.

REV. J. D. HERR, D. D.   W. W. BENTLEY.

1. Ho - ly Spir - it, hear my cry, To my soul be ev - er nigh;
2. Come, and enter now with-in, Chase a - way my fear and sin;
3. Bring to me the changeless love Of my Sav - ior, gone a - bove;

For my Lord has promised me   Com-fort-less thou shalt not be.
And the blood of Je - sus show, In   it wash me white as snow.
Be my com-fort - er and guide, Ev - er with my soul a - bide.

4 Make me love God's holy law,
   From its sacred pages draw
   Lessons Thou wouldst have me learn,
   Of my Lord, for whom I yearn.

5 Help me always to express
   The high calling I profess;
   And in Christ complete appear,
   When my race is ended here.

WE COME, A MIGHTY LEGION. Concluded.

We'll con-quer ev-'ry re-gion, For we're going to take the world.

No. 71.   MY ANCHOR IS HOLDING.

"Which hope we have as an anchor of the soul."—HEB. 6: 19.

Mrs. E. W. CHAPMAN.   J. H. TENNEY.

1. Sweet Hope, the anchor of my soul, En-ters with-in the vail;
2. My life's frail bark is oft-en tossed, High on the mountain waves,
3. Fair Heaven's dome is just in view, Beauti-ful, gold-en land!

Rests in the Sav-ior's dy-ing love; Fears not the wild-est gale.
Steadfast and sure my an-chor holds, Firm on the Rock that saves.
Soon I shall reach its gate of pearl, Walk on its shin-ing strand.

REFRAIN.

My an-chor is hold-ing, is hold-ing, With-in the vail; My an-chor is hold-ing, is hold-ing, It will not fail.

By permission.

No. 72. WAITING FOR HIS COMING.

"And they shall see the Son of man coming in the clouds of heaven with power and great glory."—Matt. 24:30.

A. B.   A. BEIRLY.

1. My soul looks in yon par-a-dise, Where saints and an-gels dwell;
2. My soul looks in yon par-a-dise, Where ma-ny man-sions are;
3. My soul looks in yon par-a-dise, Where Christ prepared a place

And there I hear a ransomed host Their songs of prais-es swell;
There not a thought of vague un-rest My hap-pi-ness shall mar;
For ev'-ry one that o-ver-comes, To see Him face to face;

I look a-gain, and lo! I see, In ec-sta-sy di-vine,
I look a-gain, and oh, I fain Would soar on wings of love,
I look a-gain, and hold-ing fast, I feel 'twill not be long,

My Sav-ior on a throne of light, In radiant beau-ty shine.
To that a-bode of end-less bliss, And dwell with Christ a-bove.
Ere I shall see His king-ly form, And sing the tri-umph song.

CHORUS.

'Tis He, the King of Glo-ry! In maj-es-ty shall come,

WAITING FOR HIS COMING. Concluded.

To gath-er all his loved and true To their e-ter-nal home.

No. 73. ETERNITY.

FANNY J. CROSBY.   MRS. M. E. WILLSON.

With Expression.

1. Deep and grand in tones sub-lime, Hear the pass-ing bells of time
2. In the ro-sy morn-ing fair, In the sul-try noon-day glare,
3. When with breaking heart we bend O'er a tried and faith-ful friend,
4. Precious word, if safe we stand On the Christian's bor-der-land,

Ring the dirge of mo-ments dead, Golden hours whose joys are fled,
In the dew-y even-ing bright, In the si-lent hush of night,
When the part-ing hour draws nigh, And we catch the last "good-bye,"
Trust-ing Him, whose lov-ing smile Lights and cheers us all the while,

Still those ceaseless bells are heard, Toll-ing, toll-ing. Hark! the word,
Still those bells of time we hear, Toll-ing, toll-ing, loud and clear,
Still those bells of time we hear, Toll-ing, toll-ing, loud and clear,
Bells of time with joy we hear, Toll-ing, toll-ing, sweet and clear,

Slow.   *Dim.*

E-ter-ni-ty, E-ter-ni-ty, E-ter-ni-ty.

Copyright, 1881, by MRS. M. E. WILLSON.

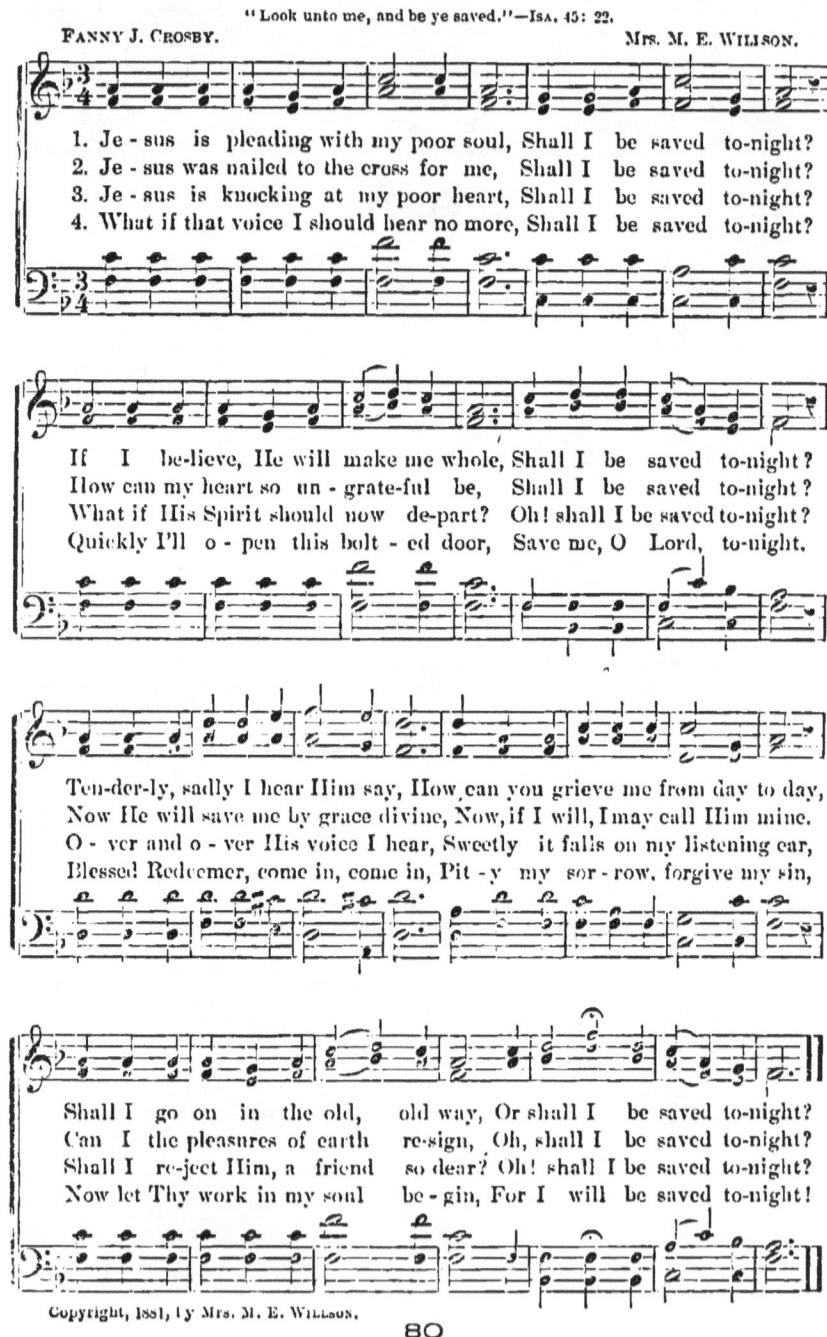

No. 75. MY SOUL IS SINGING OF JESUS.

"In my Father's house are many mansions: I go to prepare a place for you."—John 14: 2.

A. B. ALFRED BEIRLY.

1. There is a home of beau-ty, So ra-diant to be-hold, It
2. I fain would soar in rapt-ure, To mansions ev-er fair; And
3. The "meek and lowly Sav-ior," 'T was He who bore the pain; That

is the home where Je-sus dwells In splen-dor all un-told.
with the ransomed, heav'nly host A-dore my Sav-ior there!
we, through His a-ton-ing grace, Might yonder rest ob-tain!

CHORUS.

Oh, my soul is sing-ing of Je-sus, Singing of Him a-bove;

Whose precious blood on Calva-ry Was shed to make me free.

SATISFIED BY AND BY. Concluded.

By ... and by, We shall be sat-is-fied, By and by.
Safe, safe by our Savior's side,

No. 79. GATHERING ONE BY ONE.

T. C. O'K.   T. C. O'KANE.

1. { "One by one" the bonds are severed, Binding hearts together here;
   { "One by one," new ties are add-ed To the land that . . . . . .
2. { "One by one," we cease our toil-ing For the Master here be-low;
   { By the an-gel bands at-tended, To our end-less . . . . . .

CHORUS.

knows no tear. Gath'ring home, gath'ring home, "One by one," we're
rest we go.

Repeat Chorus pp.

gath'ring home; Soon we'll all be gathered home, Gathered "one by one,"

3 "One by one," we're gath'ring yonder,
   Out of ev'ry clime and land,
   "One by one," we're crossing over,
   To the distant heavenly strand.

4 "One by one," the Savior calls us
   In His perfect bliss to share;
   May we for the call be ready—
   Oh, may none be missing there!

By permission.

No. 80. UNTO HIM THAT HATH LOVED US.

REV. E. H. SMITH. H. SANDERS.

1. I have giv'n my all to Jesus, And I live where the light doth shine; In the world's deep gloom my hopes ev-er bloom, There is peace in this heart of mine.
2. I was once in darkness groping, I once roamed in the desert wild; But the Lord passed by, pouring light on my eye, And re-claimed me, his wand'ring child.
3. To the cooling fount he led me, To the pastures ev-er green; And my soul is restored, and shall boast in her Lord, For His blood hath washed me clean.

REFRAIN.
Unto him that hath loved us, and washed ev-'ry stain, Unto Him the dominion and glory be giv'n; O'er the world He shall come in His beauty to reign, As He reigns in the brightness of heav'n.

4 My faith, as the eagle, mounteth
  On her pinion bold and strong;
And the world beneath is the sadness of
  But above is immortal song. [death,

5 O swift are the moments speeding,
  And the land that is far away
Soon, soon shall be mine! and its morn-
  Will dawn an eternal day. [ing divine,

By permission.

No. 82. BLESSED ASSURANCE.

Fanny Crosby. Mrs. Jos. F. Knapp.

1. Blessed as-sur-ance, Je-sus is mine! Oh, what a fore-taste of glo-ry di-vine! Heir of sal-va-tion, purchased of God, Born of His Spir-it, washed in His blood.
2. Perfect sub-mission, per-fect de-light, Vis-ions of rapt-ure burst on my sight; Angels descend-ing, bring from a-bove, Ech-oes of mer-cy, whis-pers of love.
3. Perfect sub-mission, all is at rest, I in my Sav-ior am hap-py and blest; Watching and waiting, looking a-bove, Fill'd with His good-ness, lost in His love.

CHORUS.

This is my sto-ry, this is my song, Praising my Sav-ior all the day long; This is my sto-ry, this is my song, Prais-ing my Sav-ior all the day long.

From "Notes of Joy." By per.

No. 83. I AM SWEETLY SAVED IN JESUS.

"Who loved me, and gave Himself for me."—GAL 2: 20.

MRS. M. E. BLISS WILLSON.   W. W. BENTLEY.

1. Oh, the wondrous love that res-cued, My poor soul from guilt and sin;
2. In my wretch-ed-ness I wandered, Seek-ing thus to ease my mind,
3. 'Twas the Spirit whispered to me, That in Me thou shalt find peace;
4. I be-lieve that Je-sus saves me, Fill-ing all my soul with love,

'Twas the Spir-it gen-tly knocking, Then I op'ed the door with-in.
I had tried all earth-ly pleas-ure, But the rest I could not find.
And with earn-est-ness I plead-ed, Then and there to find re-lease.
And the praise shall be un-to Him, Both in earth and heav'n a-bove.

REFRAIN.

I am sweet-ly saved in Je - sus, Glo-ry, glo-ry fills my soul,

I am sweet-ly saved in Je - sus, And His blood has made me whole.

Copyright, 1881, by MRS. M. E. WILLSON.

No. 84. UNTO THEE WILL I CLING.

Rev. Dwight Williams.   D. B. Towner.

1. I will cling to the Cross ev-ery hour, While the surges of life round me roll, For my Sav-ior shall be my high tower, He the ref-uge and joy of my soul.
2. I will come to Thy shel-ter-ing side, Where the healing in crim-son doth flow, I will dwell near the dear Cru-ci-fied, By whose blood I am made white as snow.
3. On the Rock that is high-er than I, I will build while the waves round me roll, I will trust in the arm that is nigh, For the Lord is the strength of my soul.

CHORUS.

Un-to Thee will I cling, Thou wilt hold this poor heart which I bring; On-ly safe is the

(Bass): Un-to Thee, un-to Thee will I cling,   which I bring; On-ly safe, on-ly

By permission.   Copyright, 1878, by John Church & Co.

UNTO THEE WILL I CLING. Concluded.

way, While I trust, while I cling ev-'ry day.
safe is the way,

No. 85.   LORD, REVIVE US.

C. H. G.   CHAS. H. GABRIEL.

1. Come, dear Sav-ior, to our meet-ing, Pour a bless-ing full and
2. 'Tis for more of love we're call-ing, Of thy pre-cious love so
3. Sav-ior, draw by thy great pow-er, All our souls near un-to

free, All of Satan's plans de-feat-ing, Let us all thy presence see.
sweet, On our bended knees we're falling, At thy throne, low at thy feet.
Thee, Blessed Je-sus, kind-ly show-er, Now a blessing full and free.

CHORUS.

Lord, re-vive us, Lord, re-vive us, Of thy love give more and
more, Lord, revive us, Lord, revive us, Now a blessing we im-plore.

No. 86. MERCY FOR ALL.

FANNY J. CROSBY.   G. P. BENJAMIN.

1. We are bought with a price by the Lamb that was slain; He has conquered the grave,—he liveth a-gain! At the foot of the cross he will an-swer our call: Blessed be the Lord! there is mer-cy for all.
2. We may drink if we will of the fount-ain so free, That is flow-ing to-day for you and for me; With our bur-den of sin at its brink we may fall: Blessed be the Lord! there is mer-cy for all.
3. Oh, the rich - es of grace that in Je - sus a-bound With the full-ness of joy His peo-ple are crown'd; At the door of His love He will an - swer our call: Blessed be the Lord! there is mer-cy for all.
4. If we walk in the path that our Mas - ter has trod,—If we die un-to sin, but live un-to God, When we pass the dark vale He will an - swer our call: Blessed be the Lord! there is mer-cy for all.

REFRAIN.

Mer-cy for all! Mer-cy for all! Blessed be the Lord! there is mercy for all!

Mercy for all! Mer-cy for all! Blessed be the Lord! there is mercy for all!

No. 87.   IT IS BETTER FARTHER ON.
W. W. BENTLEY.

2 Night and day it singeth sweetly,
   Singeth, while I sit alone;
   Singeth, so the heart may hear it,
   "It is better farther on,"
   Singeth, so the heart may hear it,
   "It is better farther on."

3 Farther on, oh, how much farther?
   Count the mile stones one by one?
   No! no counting, only trusting,
   "It is better farther on,"
   No! no counting, only trusting,
   "It is better farther on."

No. 92. THERE'S A BETTER TIME A COMING.

[This piece may be sung effectively as Solo and Chorus.]

"In the fear of the Lord is strong confidence."—PROV. 14: 26.

Words and Music by J. E. RANKIN, D. D. Arr. by J. W. BISCHOFF.

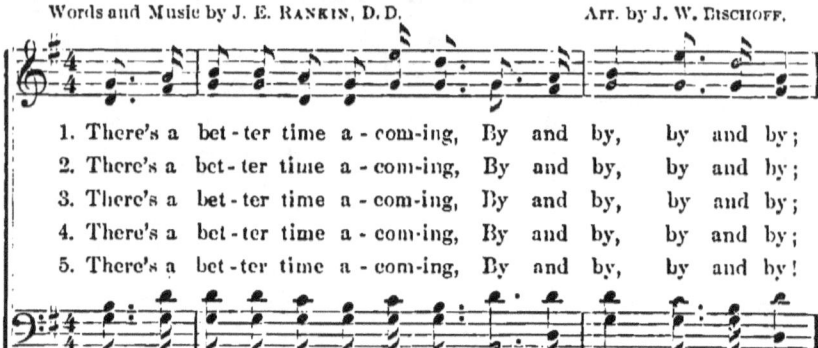

1. There's a bet-ter time a-com-ing, By and by, by and by;
2. There's a bet-ter time a-com-ing, By and by, by and by;
3. There's a bet-ter time a-com-ing, By and by, by and by;
4. There's a bet-ter time a-com-ing, By and by, by and by;
5. There's a bet-ter time a-com-ing, By and by, by and by!

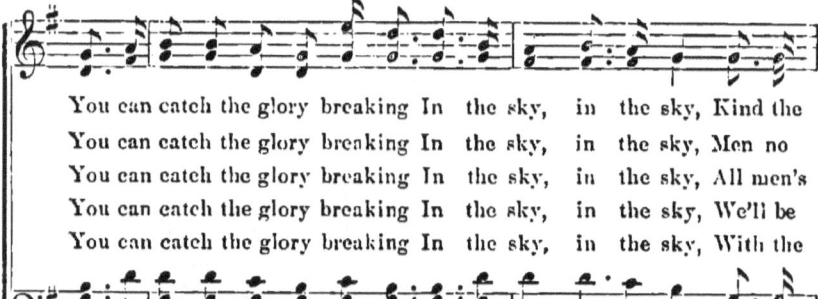

You can catch the glory breaking In the sky, in the sky, Kind the
You can catch the glory breaking In the sky, in the sky, Men no
You can catch the glory breaking In the sky, in the sky, All men's
You can catch the glory breaking In the sky, in the sky, We'll be
You can catch the glory breaking In the sky, in the sky, With the

words which shall be spoken; Lov-ing hearts no more be brok-en;
more will tempt each oth-er; Sin-ful pas-sions they will smother;
wrongs, then, love shall right them, All men's battles, love shall fight them,
true! we here de-clare it! We'll be loy-al! now we swear it!
Lord to go be-fore us, With His ban-ner float-ing o'er us,

From "Gospel Bells." By per.

THERE'S A BETTER TIME A COMING Concluded.

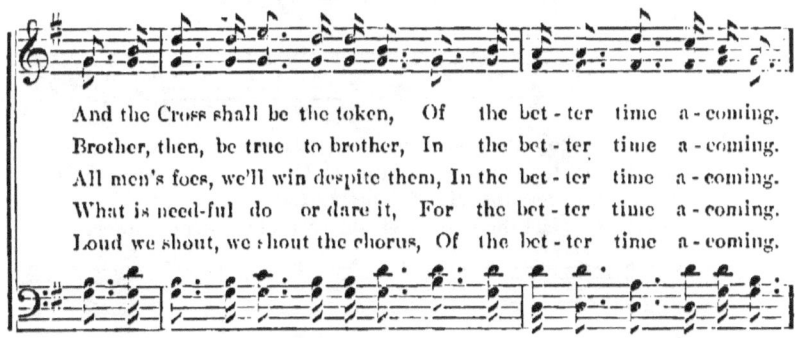

And the Cross shall be the token, Of the bet-ter time a-coming.
Brother, then, be true to brother, In the bet-ter time a-coming.
All men's foes, we'll win despite them, In the bet-ter time a-coming.
What is need-ful do or dare it, For the bet-ter time a-coming.
Loud we shout, we shout the chorus, Of the bet-ter time a-coming.

CHORUS.

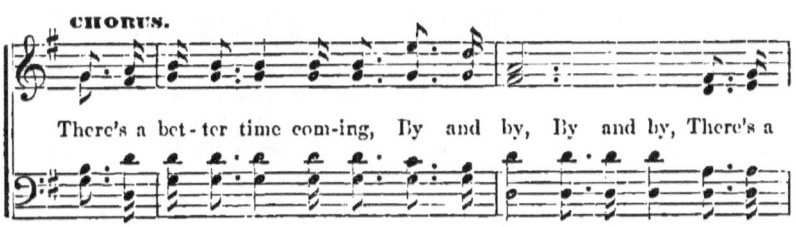

There's a bet-ter time com-ing, By and by, By and by, There's a

bet-ter time com-ing, By and by, By and by, There's a

bet-ter time coming, By and by, By and by, And you can help it on.

No. 94. ALMOST.

"Almost thou persuadest me to be a Christian."—Acts 27: 28.

MRS. O. F. WALTON.   JNO. R. SWENEY.

1. So near the door, and the door stood wide Close to the port, but not in-side! Near to the fold yet not with-in, Al-most re-solved to give up sin, Al-most per-suad-ed to count the cost, Al most a Christian, and yet lost.

2. Lord, help me trust in thy word to-day, For Thou art the Life, the Truth, the Way; Now as I come with my load of sin, The door stands open, oh help me step in, How bitter the tho't that for me at last The door should be closed, and mer-cy past.

3. Sav-ior I come—I cry un-to Thee, Oh, let not these words be true of me, I want to come to the point to-day, Oh, suf-fer me not to turn a-way; Give me no rest till my soul shall be Within the refuge—Safe in Thee.

Copyright, 1881, by Mrs. M. E. Willson.

'TWAS RUM THAT SPOILED MY BOY. Concluded.

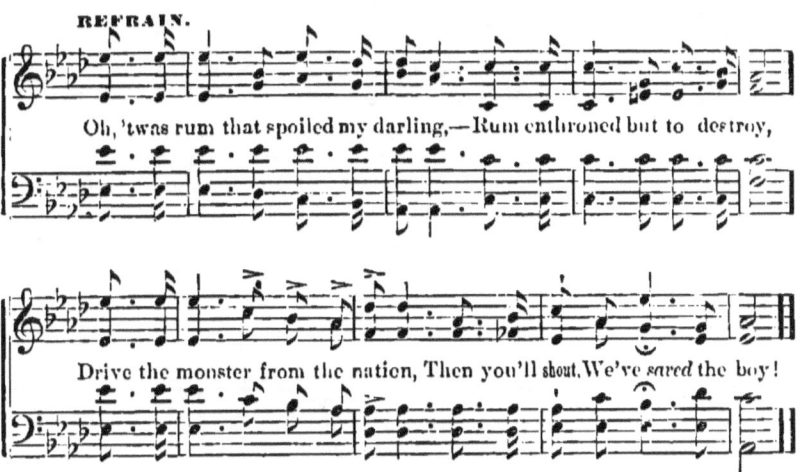

No. 96.   JESUS MY ALL.

FANNY J. CROSBY.   THEODORE E. PERKINS.

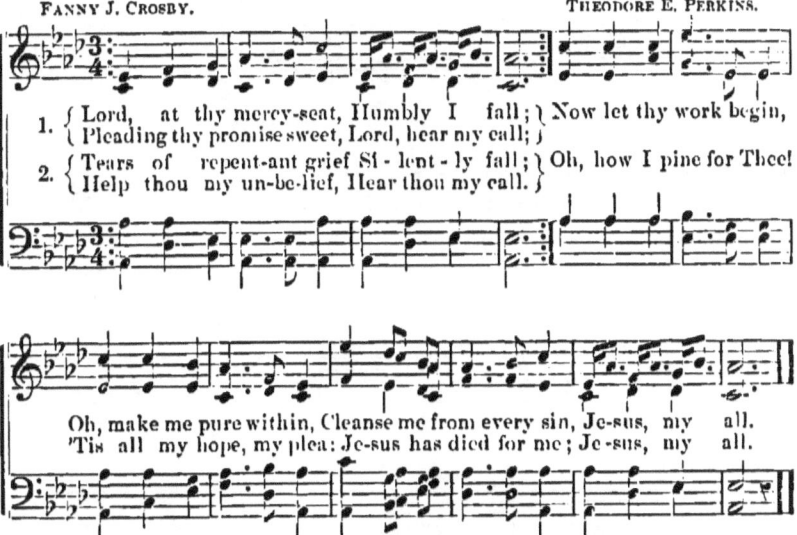

1. Lord, at thy mercy-seat, Humbly I fall; Pleading thy promise sweet, Lord, hear my call; Now let thy work begin, Oh, make me pure within, Cleanse me from every sin, Jesus, my all.

2. Tears of repent-ant grief Si-lent-ly fall; Help thou my un-be-lief, Hear thou my call. Oh, how I pine for Thee! 'Tis all my hope, my plea: Je-sus has died for me; Je-sus, my all.

3 Hark! how the words of love
   Tenderly fall,
Ere to the realms above,
   Heard is my call;
Now every doubt has flown,
Broken my heart of stone,
Lord, I am thine alone,
   Jesus, my all.

By permission.

4 Still at thy mercy-seat
   Humbly I fall;
Pleading thy promise sweet,
   Heard is my call.
Faith wings my soul to Thee,
This all my hope shall be,
Jesus has died for me,
   Jesus, my all.

WHILE THE YEARS. Concluded.

CHORUS.

Are roll-ing on, are roll-ing on, are roll-ing on, are roll-ing on,

Oh, the good we may be do-ing, While the years are roll-ing on.

No. 98.   **COME, YE DISCONSOLATE.**
"*Underneath are the everlasting arms*"—DEUT. 33: 27.

THOS. MOORE.   SAMUEL WEBBE.

1. Come, ye dis-con-so-late, where'er ye lan-guish, Come to the mer-cy-seat, fer-vent-ly kneel; Here bring your wounded hearts, here tell your an-guish, Earth has no sorrows that heav'n can not heal.
2. Joy of the des-o-late, light of the stray-ing, Hope of the pen - i - tent, fade-less and pure; Here speaks the Com-fort-er, in mer-cy say-ing, Earth has no sorrows that heav'n can not cure.
3. Here see the bread of life; see wa-ters flow-ing Forth from the throne of God, boundless in love; Come to the feast of love, come, ev-er know-ing Earth has no sorrows but heav'n can re-move.

105

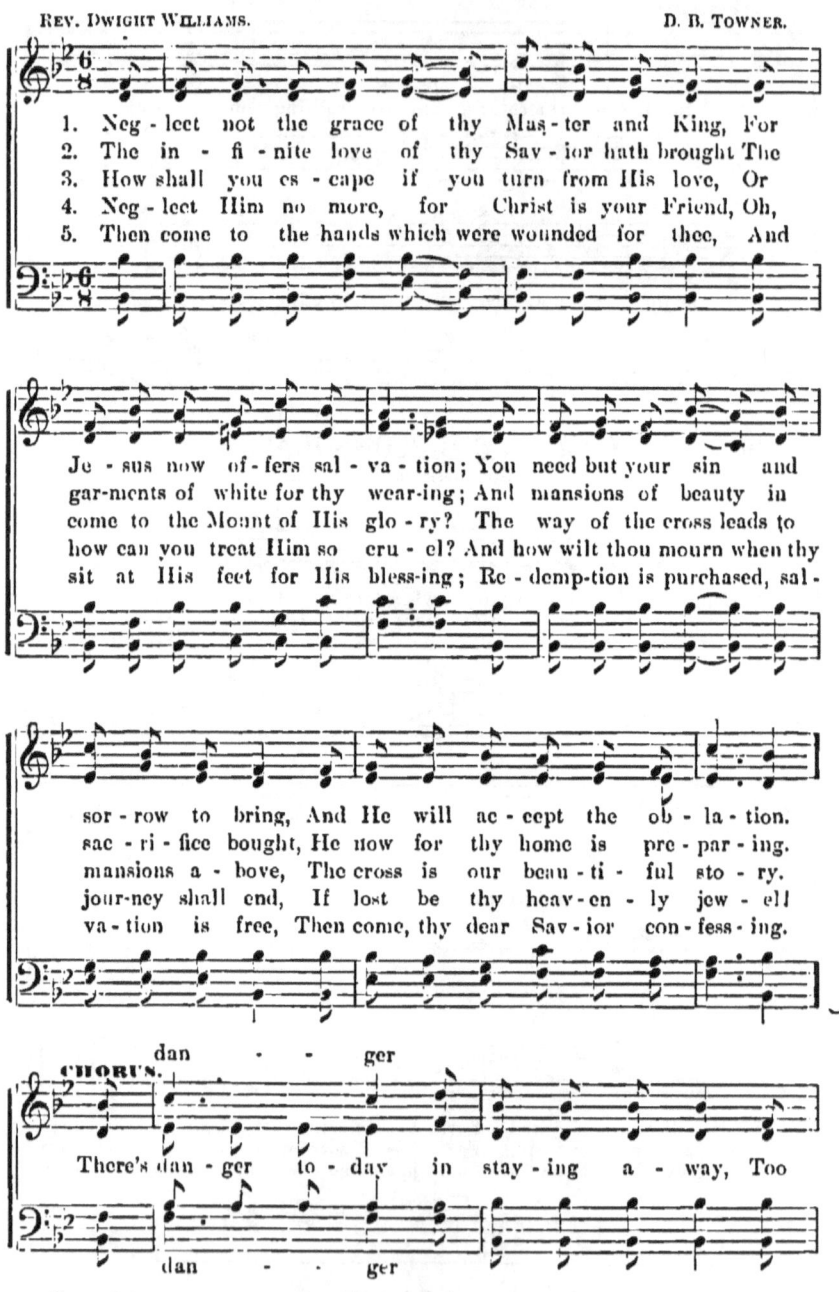

NEGLECT HIM NO MORE. Concluded.

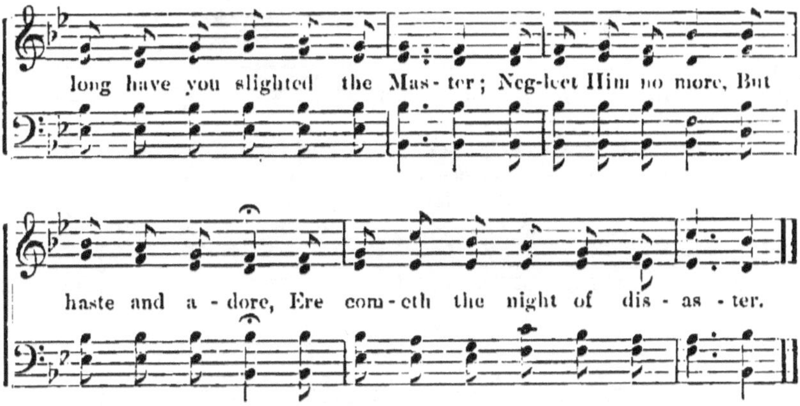

long have you slighted the Master; Neglect Him no more, But haste and adore, Ere cometh the night of disaster.

No. 100. JESUS, MEEK AND GENTLE.

H. J. SCHONACKER.

1. Jesus, meek and gentle, Son of God most high, Pitying, loving Savior, Hear thy children's cry. Pardon our offences, Loose our captive chains, Break down ev'ry idol Which our soul detains.
2. Give us holy freedom, Fill our hearts with love; Draw us, holy Jesus, To the realms above. Lead us on our journey, Be Thyself the way Thro' terrestrial darkness To celestial day.

No. 102. HE KNOWETH THE WAY I TAKE.

GEO. C. HUGG.

1. Thro' the weari-some hours of a sor-row-ful night I have pray'd for the
2. When "faint with the burden and heat of the day" I have longed for the

morning to break; Till there came—not the morn—but this broad beam of light: "He
night to o'er-take, I am rest-ed and soothed as I trust-ing-ly say, "He

knoweth the way that I take." "He knoweth the way," and the way is His own,
knoweth the way that I take." "He knoweth!" tho' toilsome, the way is His own,

And I take it with Him, not alone, not alone, And I take it with Him, not alone.

3 The road may be tangled, and thorny, and rough—
  So rough that all others forsake
And leave me discouraged; but, ah, 'tis enough!
  "He knoweth the way that I take."
"He knoweth!" though lonely, the way is His own,
And I take it with Him—not alone, not alone.

4 And so, as I journey through darkness and light
  "Till the valley's dark shades o'ertake,
And the city of rest lifts its towers on my sight,
  "He knoweth the way that I take."
"He knoweth the way!" and the way is His own,
And I take it with Him—not alone, not alone.

Copyright, 1881, by MRS. M. E. WILLSON.

No. 103. IN SIGHT OF THE CRYSTAL SEA.

"Son, remember."—Luke 15: 25.

J. E. RANKIN, D. D. J. W. BISCHOFF.

Rather slow.

1. I sat a-lone with life's mem-o-ries In sight of the crystal sea;
2. I thought me then of my childhood days, The prayer at my mother's knee:
3. I thought, I thought of the days of God, I'd wasted in fol-ly and sin—
4. I heard a voice, like the voice of God: "Remember, remember, my son!

And I saw the thrones of the star-crown'd ones, With never a crown for me.
Of the counsels grave that my father gave—The wrath I was warned to flee;
Of the times I'd mock'd when the Sav-ior knock'd, And I would not let Him in.
Re-mem-ber thy ways in the for-mer days, The crown that thou might'st have won!"

And then the voice of the Judge said "Come," Of the Judge on the great white throne;
I said, "Is it then too late, too late? Shut without, must I stand for aye?"
I thought, I thought of the vows I'd made, When I lay at death's dark door—
I thought, I thought and my thoughts ran on, Like the tide of a sun-less sea—

And I saw the star-crowned take their seats, But none could I call my own.
And the Judge, will He say, "I know you not," How-e'er I may knock and pray?
"Would He spare my life, I'd give up the strife, And serve Him for evermore."
"Am I living or dead?" to myself I said, "An end is there ne'er to be?"

5 It seemed as though I woke from a dream,
How sweet was the light of day!
Melodious sounded the Sabbath bells
From towers that were far away.
I then became as a little child,
And I wept, and wept afresh;
For the Lord had taken my heart of stone,
And given a heart of flesh.

6 Still oft I sit with life's memories,
And think of the crystal sea;
And I see the thrones of the star-crowned ones,
I know there's a crown for me.
And when the voice of the Judge says "Come,"
Of the Judge on the great white throne,
I know mid the thrones of the star-crowned ones
There's one I shall call my own.

From "Temperance Hymnal," by permission.

No. 104. HAVE YOU NOT A WORD FOR JESUS?

"My praise shall be continually of Thee."—Ps. 71: 6.

W. W. BENTLEY.

1. Have you not a word for Jesus? Will you now His love proclaim?
2. He has spoken words of blessing, Pardon, peace and love to you,
3. Have you not a word for Jesus? Some, perchance, while you are dumb,
4. Yours may be the joy and honor Some poor ransomed soul to bring,

REF. Have you not a word for Jesus? Will you now His love proclaim!

Who will speak if you are silent, You who know and love his name?
Glorious hope and gracious comfort, Strong and tender, sweet and true;
Wait and weary for your message, Hoping you will bid them come;
Jewels for the coronation Of your coming Lord and King;

Who will speak if you are silent, You who know and love His name?

You whom He hath called and chosen His own witnesses to be,
Does He hear you telling others Something of His love untold,
Never telling hidden sorrows, Ling'ring just outside the door,
Will you cast away the gladness, Thus your Master's joy to share,

D.C.

Will you tell your gracious Master, "Lord, we can not speak for Thee?"
Overflowings of thanksgiving, For His mercies manifold?
Longing for your hand to lead them Into rest for evermore.
All because a word for Jesus Seems too much for you to dare?

No. 105. THE NEW SONG.

Flora L. Best.   Jno. R. Sweney.

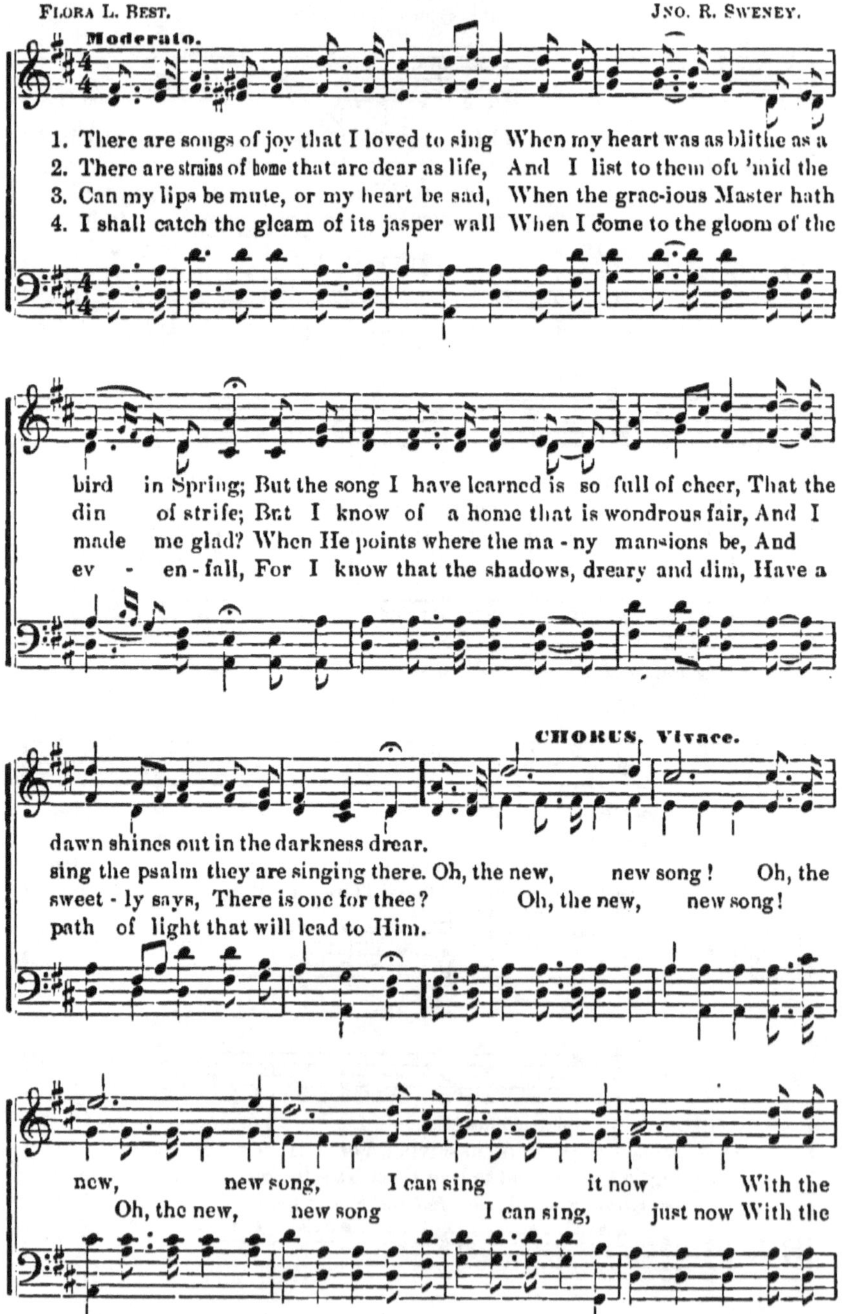

Moderato.

1. There are songs of joy that I loved to sing When my heart was as blithe as a
2. There are strains of home that are dear as life, And I list to them oft 'mid the
3. Can my lips be mute, or my heart be sad, When the gracious Master hath
4. I shall catch the gleam of its jasper wall When I come to the gloom of the

bird in Spring; But the song I have learned is so full of cheer, That the
din of strife; But I know of a home that is wondrous fair, And I
made me glad? When He points where the many mansions be, And
ev - en - fall, For I know that the shadows, dreary and dim, Have a

CHORUS, Vivace.

dawn shines out in the darkness drear.
sing the psalm they are singing there.   Oh, the new,   new song! Oh, the
sweet - ly says, There is one for thee?   Oh, the new,   new song!
path of light that will lead to Him.

new,   new song,   I can sing   it now   With the
Oh, the new,   new song   I can sing,   just now With the

From "Joy to the World," by per.

THE NEW SONG. Concluded.

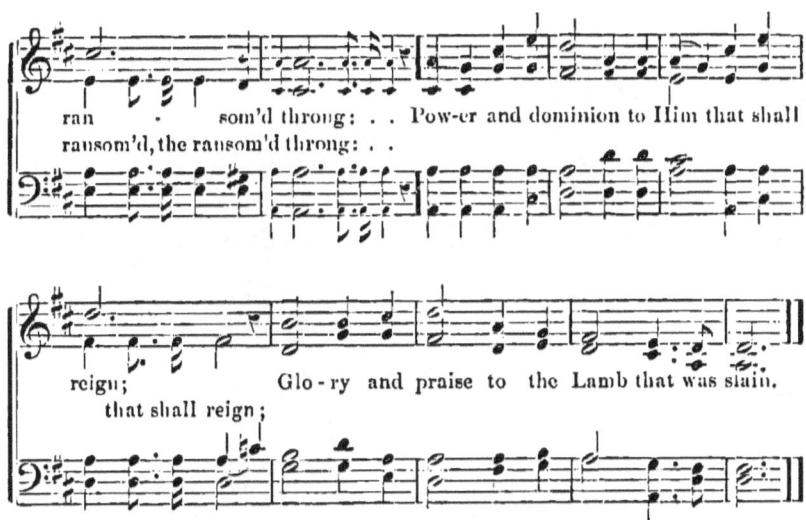

No. 106. THUS GOD DECLARES HIS SOVEREIGN WILL.

"Thou art my Son, this day have I begotten thee."—PSALM 2.

H. J. SCHONACKER.

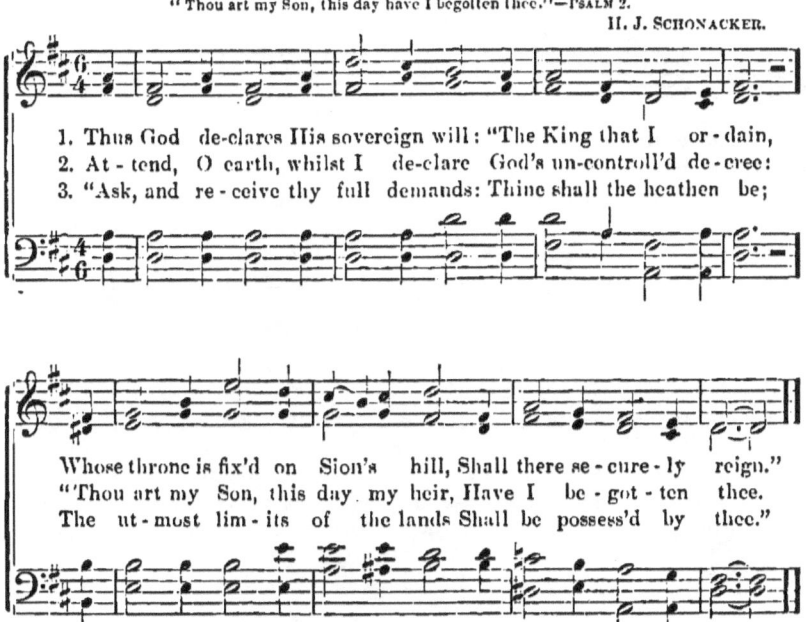

1. Thus God declares His sovereign will: "The King that I ordain,
Whose throne is fix'd on Sion's hill, Shall there securely reign."
2. Attend, O earth, whilst I declare God's uncontroll'd decree:
"Thou art my Son, this day my heir, Have I begotten thee.
3. "Ask, and receive thy full demands: Thine shall the heathen be;
The utmost limits of the lands Shall be possess'd by thee."

HOME. Concluded.

REFRAIN.

Home, where no sor-row can en-ter, Home, where no parting will be, There I shall meet at the fountain Those who are watching for me.

No. 108. ART THOU WEARY, ART THOU LANGUID?

"If any man serve me, let him follow me."

H. J. SCHONACKER.

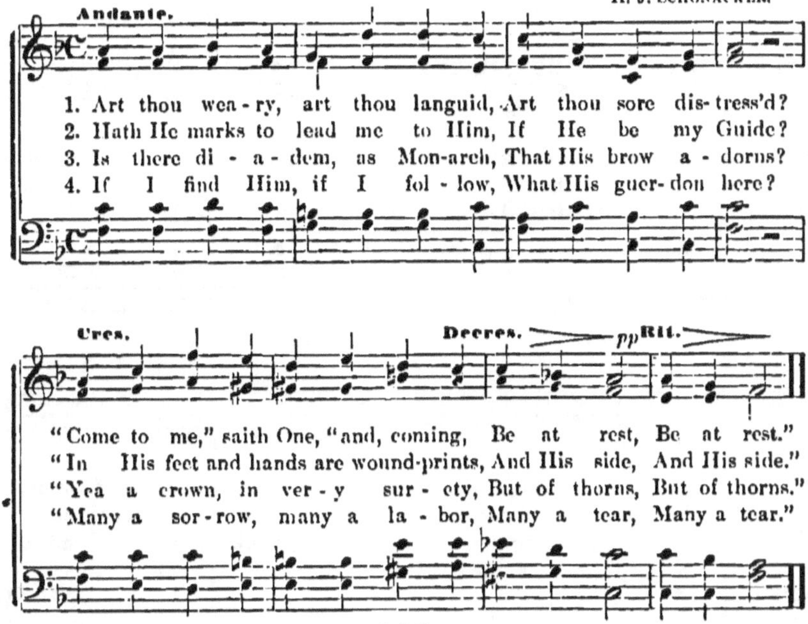

Andante.

1. Art thou wea-ry, art thou languid, Art thou sore dis-tress'd?
2. Hath He marks to lead me to Him, If He be my Guide?
3. Is there di-a-dem, as Mon-arch, That His brow a-dorns?
4. If I find Him, if I fol-low, What His guer-don here?

Cres.   *Decres.*   *pp Rit.*

"Come to me," saith One, "and, coming, Be at rest, Be at rest."
"In His feet and hands are wound-prints, And His side, And His side."
"Yea a crown, in ver-y sur-ety, But of thorns, But of thorns."
"Many a sor-row, many a la-bor, Many a tear, Many a tear."

"Singing and making melody in your heart to the Lord."—EPH. 5:19.

M. E. B. W.
M. E. BLISS WILLSON.

Joy.

1. Joy! joy! joy! I will sing for the Sav-ior has come,
2. Joy! joy-ous-ly sing, for sweet comfort He brings,
3. Joy! joy! He a-bides in my heart day by day,
4. Joy! joy! I will tell, and with joy I will sing,

To re-move all my doubts, all my fears and my gloom,
I am trust-ing Him ful-ly, I'm un-der His wing,
My "Bright Morning Star," shin-ing clear on my way,
Till oth-er poor sin-ners to Je-sus I'll bring;

He light-ens and com-forts my once-bur-dened heart,
His Spir-it di-vine fills my soul with the song,
His pow-er is so great, that now I can rest,
His love is so bound-less, so full and so free,

Rit.

And from His bright presence I nev-er will part.
His sal-va-tion is mine, and to Him I be-long.
Trust-ing all to His care, I lean on His breast.
That all may be saved if they trust Him like me.

Copyright, 1881, by M. E. Willson.

117

No. 112. SATISFIED.

Rev. J. Parker. Mrs. Joseph F. Knapp.

1. I shall not want, Hal-le-lu-jah! For God is the sun of my life, My shield to pro-tect me from dan-ger, Whenev-er I'm press'd in the strife.
2. I shall not want, He's my shepherd, The weakest are safe in His care, Lamb-like, I re-pose on His bo-som, He loves me, I've noth-ing to fear.
3. I shall not want, I am hiding, Like a bird beat'n back by the blast, In His shelt'ring love still con-fid-ing, I rest till all dan-ger is past.
4. I shall not want, O how oft-en He sendeth me help from above, Men trust to themselves in pro-vid-ing, But I in His boun-ti-ful love.

REFRAIN.

I'm sat-is-fied, yes, sat-is-fied God is my rest,
O I'm sat-is-fied, sat-is-fied, God is my rest.

5
I shall not want, every murmur
Is hushed by the sound of His voice,
And though I may pass thro' the furnace,
I lean on His arm and rejoice.
Cho.—I'm satisfied, etc.

6
I shall not want, in the valley,
Where shadows of death gather round,
The morning of heaven will greet me,
And gladness and glory abound.
Cho.—I'm satisfied, etc.

By permission.

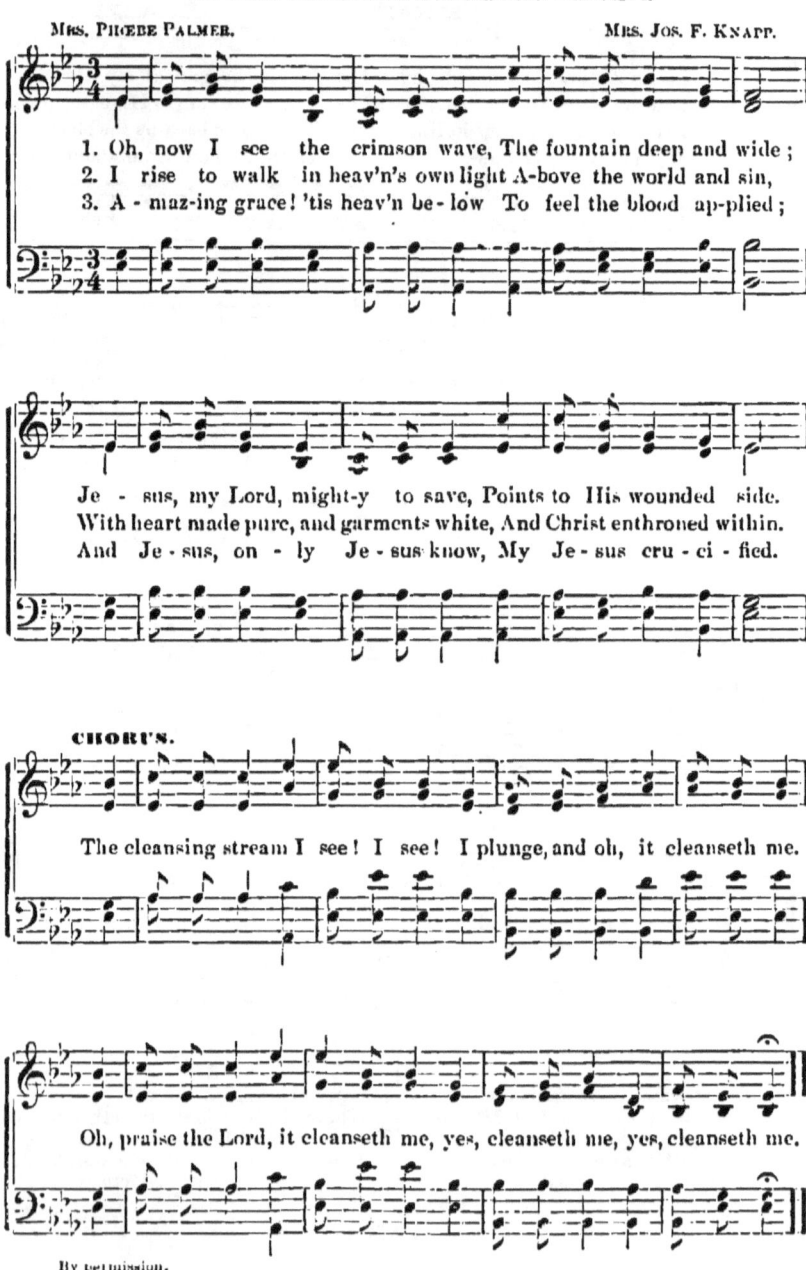

No. 114. **SEND ME.**

"Here am I, send me."—Isaiah 6:8.

K. M., Jr.   Rev. K. MACKENZIE, Jr.

1. I have heard my Sav-ior call-ing To the har-vest rich and fair; Where the workmen now are bus-y, I must take my sta-tion there.
2. Or, per-haps, there may be stand-ing, Hid a-mong the weeds of sin, Gold-en grain to grace the gar-ner, Which the lab'rers have not seen.
3. Yes, I'm read-y for His serv-ice, In my gra-cious Mas-ter's name I'll de-vote my ev-'ry tal-ent, That He may His lost re-claim.
4. Precious Sav-ior, be Thou near me, Help my light to hum-bly shine; Let Thy blessed presence cheer me With the rays of light di-vine.

CHO. Yes! I'm go-ing, Je-sus calls me, And I has-ten now to be One a-mong His faithful fol'wers: "Here am I, O Lord, send me."

Though I may not with the reap-ers Gath-er large and heav-y sheaves, I, like Ruth, may catch stray handfuls Which some careless gleaner leaves.
These are mine to speak of Je-sus, Mine to point the way a-bove, Mine to car-ry with thanksgiving To the Sav-ior's arms of love.
These my hands and feet shall la-bor; This my heart His all shall be, While my lips exclaim with rapture, "Here am I, O Lord, send me."
Though my ef-forts may be fee-ble Sin-ful hearts to win to Thee, Thou wilt give me grace to tell them, "Jesus says, 'Come un-to me.'"

D. C.

Copyright, 1881, by K. MACKENZIE, JR.

No. 115. COME TO THE CROSS.

Mrs. E. C. Ellsworth.   P. P. Bliss.

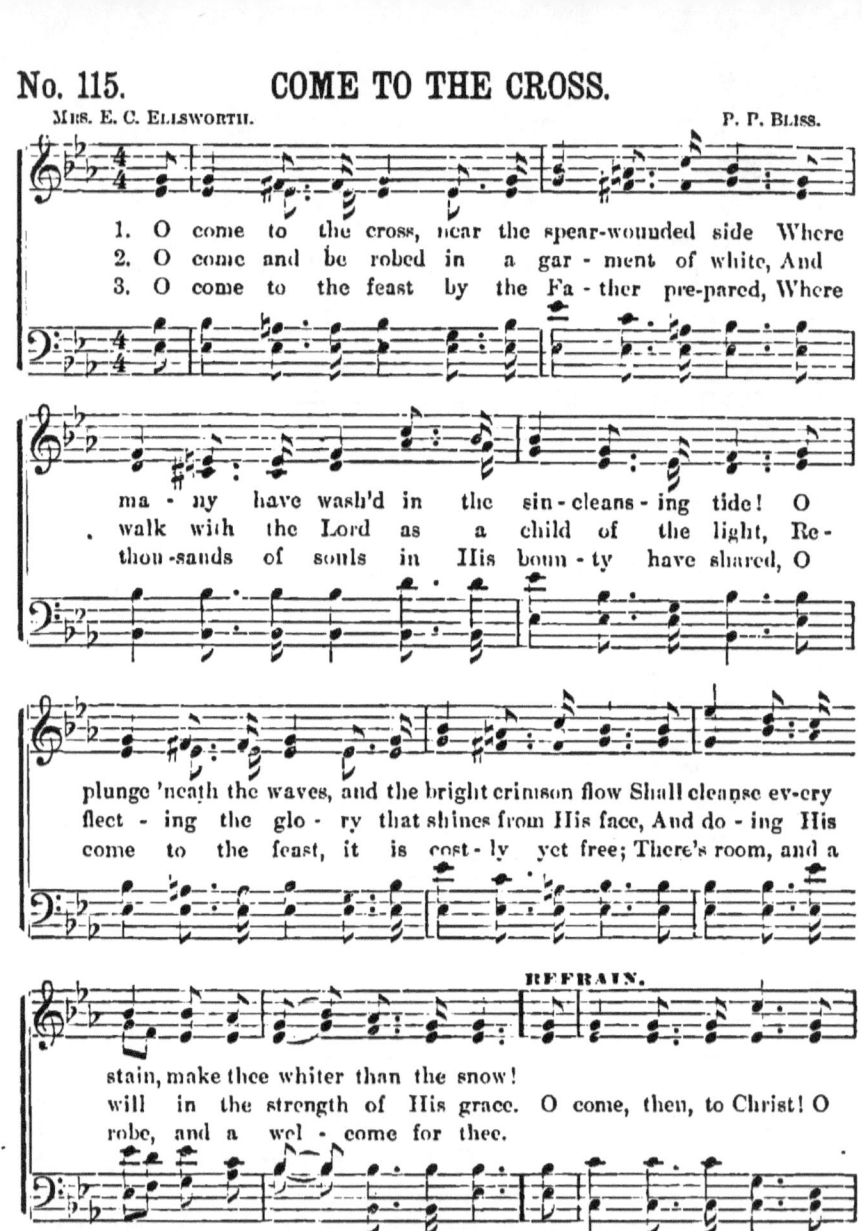

1. O come to the cross, near the spear-wounded side Where many have wash'd in the sin-cleansing tide! O plunge 'neath the waves, and the bright crimson flow Shall cleanse ev-ery stain, make thee whiter than the snow!
2. O come and be robed in a garment of white, And walk with the Lord as a child of the light, Reflecting the glory that shines from His face, And doing His will in the strength of His grace.
3. O come to the feast by the Father prepared, Where thousands of souls in His bounty have shared, O come to the feast, it is costly yet free; There's room, and a robe, and a welcome for thee.

REFRAIN.

O come, then, to Christ! O come, come to-day! He'll save thee, He'll wash all thy stains of sin a-way.

FAMILIAR HYMNS.

No. 118. Tune—MARTYN. Key F.

1. Jesus! lover of my soul,
    Let me to thy bosom fly,
While the nearer waters roll,
    While the tempest still is high;
Hide me, O my Savior, hide,
    Till the storm of life be past;
Safe into the haven guide—
    O receive my soul at last!

2. Other refuge have I none;
    Hangs my helpless soul on thee;
Leave, ah! leave me not alone;
    Still support and comfort me.
All my trust on thee is stayed:
    All my help from thee I bring;
Cover my defenseless head
    With the shadow of thy wing.

3. Plenteous grace with thee is found—
    Grace to cover all my sin;
Let the healing streams abound,
    Make and keep me pure within.
Thou of life the fountain art;
    Freely let me take of thee:
Spring thou up within my heart,
    Rise to all eternity.

—o—

No. 119. Tune—"I GAVE MY LIFE FOR THEE." Key C.

1. I gave my life for thee,
    My precious blood I shed,
That thou might'st ransomed be,
    And quickened from the dead;
I gave, I gave my life for thee,
What hast thou given for me?

2. My Father's house of light,—
    My glory circled throne,
I left, for earthly night,
    For wand'rings sad and lone;
I left, I left it all for thee;
Hast thou left aught for me?

3. I suffered much for thee,
    More than thy tongue can tell
Of bitterest agony,
    To rescue thee from hell;
I've borne, I've borne it all for thee,
What hast thou borne for me?

4. And I have brought to thee,
    Down from my home above,
Salvation full and free,
    My pardon and my love;
I bring, I bring rich gifts to thee,
What hast thou brought to me?

No. 120. Tune—THE GREAT PHYSICIAN. Key E♭.

1. The great physician now is near,
    The sympathizing Jesus;
He speaks the drooping heart to cheer,
    Oh, hear the voice of Jesus.

Cho.—Sweetest note in seraph song,
    Sweetest name on mortal tongue,
Sweetest carol ever sung,
    Jesus, blessed Jesus.

2. Your many sins are all forgiven,
    Oh, hear the voice of Jesus;
Go on your way in peace to heaven,
    And wear a crown with Jesus.

3. All glory to the dying Lamb!
    I now believe in Jesus;
I love the blessed Savior's name,
    I love the name of Jesus.

4. His name dispels my guilt and fear,
    No other name but Jesus;
Oh, how my soul delights to hear
    The precious name of Jesus.

5. And when to that bright world above,
    We rise to see our Jesus,
We'll sing around the throne of love
    His name, the name of Jesus.

—o—

No. 121. Tune—BETHANY. Key G.

1. Nearer, my God, to Thee,
    Nearer to Thee!
E'en though it be a cross
    That raiseth me;
Still all my song shall be—
Nearer, my God, to Thee!
    Nearer to Thee!

2. Though, like the wanderer,
    The sun gone down,
Darkness be over me,
    My rest a stone;
Yet in my dreams I'd be—
Nearer, my God, to Thee!
    Nearer to Thee!

3. There let the way appear,
    Steps unto heaven;
All that Thou sendest me,
    In mercy given;
Angels to beckon me—
Nearer, my God, to Thee!
    Nearer to Thee!

No. 122. Tune—ARLINGTON. Key G.

1. Am I a soldier of the cross,—
A follower of the Lamb,—
And shall I fear to own his cause,
Or blush to speak his name?

2. Are there no foes for me to face?
Must I not stem the flood?
Is this vile world a friend to grace,
To help me on to God?

3. Sure I must fight if I would reign;
Increase my courage, Lord!
I'll bear the toil, endure the pain,
Supported by thy word.

—o—

No. 123. Tune—DENNIS S. M. Key G

1. Blest be the tie that binds
Our hearts in Christian love;
The fellowship of kindred minds
Is like to that above

2. Before our Father's throne,
We pour our ardent prayers; [one,
Our fears, our hopes, our aims are
Our comforts and our cares.

3. We share our mutual woes;
Our mutual burdens bear;
And often for each other flows
The sympathizing tear.

—o—

No. 124. Tune—BALERMA. Key B♭.

1. Dear Father, to thy mercy-seat
My soul for shelter flies:
'Tis here I find a safe retreat
When storms and tempests rise.

2. My cheerful hope can never die,
If thou, my God, art near;
Thy grace can raise my comforts high,
And banish every fear.

3. Oh, never let my soul remove
From this divine retreat!
Still let me trust thy power and love,
And dwell beneath thy feet.

—o—

No. 125. Tune—CORONATION. Key G.

1. All hail the power of Jesus' name,
Let angels prostrate fall;
Bring forth the royal diadem,
And crown him—Lord of all.

2. Let high-born seraphs tune the lyre,
And as they tune it, fall
Before his face, who tunes their choir,
And crown him—Lord of all.

3. Ye seed of Israel's chosen race,
Ye ransomed of the fall;
Hail him who saves you by his grace,
And crown him—Lord of all.

4. Sinners! whose love can ne'er forget,
The wormwood and the gall,
Go, spread your trophies at his feet,
And crown him—Lord of all.

—o—

No. 126. Tune—THE MISTAKES OF MY LIFE. Key G.

1. The mistakes of my life have been many,
The sins of my heart have been more,
And I scarce can see for weeping,
But I'll knock at the open door.

Cho.—I know I am weak and sinful,
It comes to me more and more;
But when the dear Savior shall bid me come in,
I'll enter the open door.

2. I am lowest of those who love Him,
I am weakest of those who pray;
But I come as He has bidden,
And He will not say me nay.

3. My mistakes His free grace will cover,
My sins He will wash away,
And the feet that shrink and falter
Shall walk thro' the gates of day.

4. The mistakes of my life have been many,
And my spirit is sick with sin,
And I scarce can see for weeping,
But the Savior will let me in.

—o—

No. 127. Tune—TO-DAY THE SAVIOR CALLS. Key F.

1. To-day the Savior calls:
Ye wand'rers come;
O, ye benighted souls,
Why longer roam?

2. To-day the Savior calls:
Oh, listen now;
Within these sacred walls
To Jesus bow.

3. To-day the Savior calls:
For refuge fly;
The storm of justice falls,
And death is nigh.

4. The Spirit calls to-day:
Yield to his power;
Oh, grieve Him not away;
'Tis mercy's hour.

No. 128. Tune—ROCK OF AGES.
Key B♭.

1. Rock of Ages, cleft for me,
Let me hide myself in thee ;
Let the water and the blood,
From thy wounded side which flow'd,
Be of sin the double cure,—
Save from wrath and make me pure.

2. Could my tears forever flow,
Could my zeal no languor know,
These for sin could not atone ;
Thou must save, and thou alone :
In my hand no price I bring ;
Simply to the cross I cling.

3. While I draw this fleeting breath,
When my eyes shall close in death,
When I rise to worlds unknown,
And behold thee on thy throne
Rock of Ages, cleft for me,
Let me hide myself in thee.

—o—

No. 129. Tune—OVER THERE.
Key A♯.

1. Oh, think of the home over there,
By the side of the river of light,
Where the saints all immortal and fair,
Are robed in their garments of white.

REF.—Over there, over there,
Oh, think of the home over there.

2. Oh, think of the friends over there,
Who before us the journey have trod,
Of the songs that they breathe on the air,
In their home in the palace of God.

REF.—Over there, over there,
Oh, think of the friends over there.

3. My Savior is now over there, [rest ;
There my kindred and friends are at
Then away from my sorrow and care,
Let me fly to the land of the blest.

Over there, over there,
My Savior is now over there.

—o—

No. 130. Tune—WELTON. L. M.
Key B♭.

1. Return, O wanderer, return,
And seek thy Father's face ;
Those new desires which in thee b
Were kindled by his grace.

2. Return, O wanderer, return,
Thy Savior bids thee live :
Come to his cross, and, grateful, learn
How freely he'll forgive.

3. Return, O wanderer, return ;
Regain thy long-sought rest :
The Savior's melting mercies yearn
To clasp thee to his breast.

No. 131. Tune—PRECIOUS PROMISE.
Key G.

1. Precious promise God hath given
To the weary passer by,
On the way from earth to heaven,
"I will guide thee with Mine eye."

REF.—I will guide thee, I will guide thee,
I will guide thee with Mine eye ;
On the way from earth to heaven
I will guide thee with Mine eye.

2. When temptations almost win thee,
And thy trusted watchers fly ;
Let this promise ring within thee,
"I will guide thee with Mine eye."

3. When thy secret hopes have perished,
In the grave of years gone by ;
Let this promise still be cherished,
"I will guide thee with Mine eye."

4. When the shades of life are falling,
And the hour has come to die ;
Hear thy trusty Pilot calling,
"I will guide thee with Mine eye."

—o—

No. 132. Tune—BALERMA.
Key B♭.

1. Forever here my rest shall be,
Close to thy bleeding side :
This all my hope, and all my plea,
For me the Savior died!

2. My dying Savior, and my God,
Fountain for guilt and sin,
Sprinkle me over with thy blood,
And cleanse, and keep me clean.

3. Wash me, and make me thus thine
Wash me, and mine thou art ; [own ;
Wash me, but not my feet alone,
My hands, my head, my heart.

4. The atonement of thy blood apply,
Till faith to sight improve ;
Till hope in full fruition die,
And all my soul be love.

—o—

No. 133. Tune—WE'LL STAND THE STORM.
Key G.

1. When I can read my title clear
To mansions in the skies,
I'll bid farewell to every fear,
And wipe my weeping eyes.

CHO.—We will stand the storm,
We will anchor by and by.

2. Let cares like a wild deluge come,
And storms of sorrow fall,
May I but safely reach my home,
My God, my heaven, my all !

3. There shall I bathe my weary soul
In seas of heavenly rest,
And not a wave of trouble roll
Across my peaceful breast.

No. 134. Tune—WHITER THAN SNOW,
Key A♭.

1. Dear Jesus, I long to be perfectly
   whole;
I want thee forever to live in my soul;
Break down every idol, cast out every
   foe;   [snow.
Now wash me, and I shall be whiter than

Whiter than snow, yes, whiter than
   snow,
Now wash me, and I shall be whiter than
   snow.

2. Dear Jesus, let nothing unholy re-
   main;   [stain;
Apply thine own blood and extract every
To have this blest cleansing, I all things
   forego;   [snow.
Now wash me and I shall be whiter than

3. The blessing by faith I receive from
   above,   [love;
O, glory! my soul is made perfect in
My prayer has prevailed, and this mo-
   ment I know   [snow.
The blood is applied—I am whiter than

—o—

No. 135. Tune—WHAT A FRIEND IN JESUS.
Key F.

1. What a friend we have in Jesus,
   All our sins and griefs to bear;
What a privilege to carry
   Every thing to God in prayer.
Oh, what peace we often forfeit,
   Oh, what needless pain we bear—
All because we do not carry
   Everything to God in prayer.

2. Have we trials and temptations?
   Is there trouble anywhere?
We should never be discouraged,
   Take it to the Lord in prayer.
Can we find a Friend so faithful,
   Who will all our sorrows share?
Jesus knows our every weakness,
   Take it to the Lord in prayer.

3. Are we weak and heavy laden,
   Cumbered with a load of care?
Precious Savior, still our refuge,
   Take it to the Lord in prayer.
Do thy friends despise, forsake thee?
   Take it to the Lord in prayer;
In His arms He'll take and shield thee,
   Thou wilt find a solace there.

—o—

No. 136. Tune—OLIVET.
Key E♭.

1. My faith looks up to thee,
   Thou Lamb of Calvary;
   Savior divine;
Now hear me while I pray;
Take all my guilt away;
Oh let me, from this day,
   Be wholly thine.

2. May thy rich grace impart,
   Strength to my fainting heart;
   My zeal inspire;
As thou hast died for me,
Oh may my love to thee,
Pure, warm and changeless be—
   A living fire.

3. While life's dark maze I tread,
   And grief around me spread,
   Be thou my guide;
Bid darkness turn to day;
Wipe sorrow's tears away
Nor let me ever stray
   From thee aside.

—o—

No. 137. Tune—SHALL WE MEET BEYOND THE
RIVER? Key A.

1. Shall we meet beyond the river,
   Where the surges cease to roll?
Where, in all the bright forever,
   Sorrow ne'er shall press the soul?

CHO.—Shall we meet, shall we meet,
   Shall we meet beyond the river?
Shall we meet beyond the river,
   Where the surges cease to roll?

2. Shall we meet in that blest harbor
   When our stormy voyage is o'er?
Shall we meet and cast the anchor
   By the fair, celestial shore?

3. Shall we meet in yonder city,
   Where the tow'rs of crystal shine?
Where the walls are all of jasper,
   Built by workmanship divine?

—o—

No. 138. Tune—FOUNTAIN.
Key C.

1. There is a fountain filled with blood,
   Drawn from Immanuel's veins,
And sinners plunged beneath that flood
   Lose all their guilty stains.

2. The dying thief rejoiced to see
   That fountain in his day;
And there may I, though vile as he,
   Wash all my sins away.

3. Thou dying Lamb! thy precious
   Shall never lose its power,   [blood
Till all the ransomed Church of God
   Are saved to sin no more.

4. E'er since by faith I saw the stream
   Thy flowing wounds supply,
Redeeming love has been my theme,
   And shall be till I die.

5. Then in a nobler, sweeter song
   I'll sing Thy power to save,   [tongue
When this poor, lisping, stammering
   Lies silent in the grave.

No. 139. Tune—NINETY AND NINE.
Key A♭.

1. There were ninety and nine that safe-
   In the shelter of the fold, [ly lay
   But one was out on the hills away,
   Far off from the gates of gold—
   Away on the mountains wild and bare,
   Away from the tender Shepherd's care.

2. "Lord, thou hast here thy ninety and
   nine:
   Are they not enough for thee?"
   But the Shepherd made answer: "This
   of mine
   Has wandered away from me:
   And although the road be rough and
   steep,
   I go to the desert to find my sheep."

3. But none of the ransomed ever knew
   How deep were the waters crossed;
   Nor how dark was the night that the
   Lord passed through
   Ere he found his sheep that was lost.
   Out in the desert he heard its cry—
   Sick and helpless, and ready to die.

4. But all through the mountains, thun-
   der-riven,
   And up from the rocky steep,
   There rose a cry to the gate of heaven,
   "Rejoice! I have found my sheep!"
   And the angels echoed around the
   throne, [own!"
   "Rejoice, for the Lord brings back his

—o—

No. 140. Tune—WHAT SHALL THE HARVEST BE? Key C.

1. Sowing the seed by the day-light fair,
   Sowing the seed by the noon-day glare,
   Sowing the seed by the fading light,
   Sowing the seed in the solemn night,
   ‖:Oh, what shall the harvest be?:‖

Cho.—Sown in the darkness or sown in
   the light, [might,
   Sown in our weakness or sown in our
   Gathered in time or eternity. [be.
   Sure, ah, sure will the harvest, harvest

2. Sowing the seed by the way-side high,
   Sowing the seed on the rock to die,
   Sowing the seed where the thorns will
   spoil,
   Sowing the seed in the fertile soil,
   ‖:Oh, what shall the harvest be?:‖

3. Sowing the seed with an aching heart,
   Sowing the seed while the teardrops
   start,
   Sowing in hope till the reapers come
   Gladly to gather the harvest home,
   ‖:Oh, what shall the harvest be?:‖

No. 141. Tune—REST FOR THE WEARY.
Key G.

1. In the Christian's home in glory,
   There remains a land of rest,
   Where the Savior's gone before me
   To fulfill my soul's request.

Cho.—On the other side of Jordan,
   In the sweet fields of Eden,
   Where the tree of life is blooming,
   There is rest for you.
   There is rest for the weary,
   There is rest for you.

2. Pain or sickness ne'er can enter;
   Grief nor woe my lot shall share;
   But in that celestial center
   I, a crown of life shall wear.

3. Sing, O sing, ye heirs of glory,
   Shout your triumph as you go;
   Zion's gates will open to you,
   You shall find an entrance through.

—o—

No. 142. Tune—HE LEADETH ME.
Key D.

1. He leadeth me! oh, blessed thought;
   Oh! words with heav'nly comfort fraught;
   Whate'er I do, where'er I be,
   Still 'tis God's hand that leadeth me.

Ref.—He leadeth me, He leadeth me!
   By his own hand he leadeth me;
   His faithful follower I would be,
   For by his hand he leadeth me.

2. Sometimes 'mid scenes of deepest
   gloom,
   Sometimes where Eden's bowers bloom,
   By waters still, o'er troubled sea,—
   Still 'tis his hand that leadeth me.

3. Lord, I would clasp thy hand in mine,
   Nor ever murmur nor repine—
   Content, whatever lot I see,
   Since 'tis my God that leadeth me.

—o—

No. 143. Tune—WHITE AS SNOW.
Key C.

1. What! "lay my sins on Jesus?"
   God's well-beloved Son?
   No! 'tis a truth most precious,
   That God e'en *that* has done.

Cho.—Hallelujah, Jesus saves me,
   He makes me "white as snow."
   Hallelujah, Jesus saves me,
   He makes me "white as snow."

2. Yes, 'tis a truth most precious,
   To all who do believe,
   God laid our sins on Jesus,
   Who did the load receive.

3. What! "bring our guilt to Jesus?"
   To wash away our stains;
   The act is passed that freed us,
   And naught to do remains.

No. 144. Tune—COME THOU FOUNT.
Key D.

1. Come thou fount of every blessing,
   Tune my heart to sing thy grace;
Streams of mercy, never ceasing,
   Call for songs of loudest praise,
Teach me some melodious sonnet,
   Sung by flaming tongues above;
Praise the mount—I'm fixed upon it,
   Mount of thy redeeming love.

2. Here I'll raise mine Ebenezer;
   Hither by thy help I'm come;
And I hope by thy good pleasure,
   Safely to arrive at home.
Jesus sought me when a stranger,
   Wand'ring from the fold of God;
He, to rescue me from danger,
   Interposed his precious blood.

3. Oh, to grace how great a debtor
   Daily I'm constrained to be!
Let thy goodness like a fetter,
   Bind my wand'ring heart to thee.
Prone to wander, Lord, I feel it—
   Prone to leave the God I love;
Here's my heart, oh take and seal it—
   Seal it for thy courts above.

—o—

No. 145. Tune—O, HAPPY DAY.
Key G.

1. O happy day, that fixed my choice
   On Thee, my Savior and my God!
Well may this glowing heart rejoice,
   And tell its raptures all abroad.

Cho.—Happy day, happy day,
   When Jesus washed my sins away,
He taught me how to watch and pray,
   And live rejoicing every day;
Happy day, happy day,
   When Jesus washed my sins away.

2. 'Tis done, the great transaction's done—
   I am my Lord's, and He is mine;
He drew me, and I followed on,
   Charmed to confess the voice divine.

3. Now rest, my long-divided heart:
   Fixed on this blissful centre, rest;
Nor ever from thy Lord depart,
   With Him of every good possessed.

4. High heaven, that heard the solemn vow,
   That vow renewed, shall daily hear,
Till in life's latest hour I bow,
   And bless in death, a bond so dear.

—o—

No. 146. Tune—LENNOX.
Key B♭.

1. Arise, my soul, arise;
   Shake off thy guilty fears;
The bleeding Sacrifice
   In my behalf appears;
Before the throne my Surety stands,
My name is written on his hands.

2. The Father hears him pray,
   His dear anointed one:
He can not turn away
   The presence of his Son:
His Spirit answers to the blood,
And tells me I am born of God.

3. My God is reconciled,
   His pard'ning voice I hear;
He owns me for his child,
   I can no longer fear;
With confidence I now draw nigh,
And Father, Abba, Father, cry.

—o—

No. 147. Tune—CONSECRATION.
Key A♭.

1. Take my life and let it be
Consecrated, Lord, to thee.
Take my hands and let them move
At the impulse of thy love.

REFRAIN.

Take myself and let me be
Ever only all for thee.

2. Take my moments and my days,
Let them flow in ceaseless praise.
Take my will and make it thine,
Let it be no longer mine.

3. Take my heart, it is thine own,
Let it be thy royal throne.
Take my love, my Lord of power,
At thy feet its treasures store.

—o—

No. 148. Tune — TELL ME THE OLD, OLD STORY. Key C.

1. Tell me the old, old story,
   Of unseen things above;
Of Jesus and his glory,
   Of Jesus and his love.
Tell me the story simply,
   As to a little child;
For I am weak and weary,
   And helpless and defiled.

Cho.—Tell me the old, old story,
   Of Jesus and his love.

2. Tell me the story slowly,
   That I may take it in;
That wonderful redemption,
   God's remedy for sin.
Tell me the story often,
   For I forget so soon,
The "early dew" of morning
   Has passed away at noon.

3. Tell me the story softly,
   With earnest tones, and grave;
Remember, I'm the sinner
   Whom Jesus came to save;
Tell me the story always,
   If you would really be
In any time of trouble
   A comforter to me.

No. 149. Tune—DISMISSION. Key F.

1. Lord, dismiss us with thy blessing;
Fill our hearts with joy and peace;
Let us each, thy love possessing,
Triumph in redeeming grace;
Oh refresh us,
Traveling through this wilderness.

2. Thanks we give, and adoration,
For thy gospel's joyful sound;
May the fruits of thy salvation
In our hearts and lives abound;
May thy presence
With us evermore be found.

3. So, whene'er the signal's given,
Us from earth to call away,
Borne on angel's wings to heaven,
Glad the summons to obey,
May we ever
Reign with Christ in endless day.

No. 150. Tune—UNDER THE BLOOD. Key B♭.

1. I stand all bewildered with wonder,
And gaze on the ocean of love;
And over its waves to my spirit
Come peace, like a heavenly dove.

Cho.—The cross now covers my sins,
The past is under the blood;
I'm trusting in Jesus for all,
My will is the will of my God.

2. I struggled and wrestled to win it,
The blessing that setteth me free;
But when I had ceased from my struggles,
His peace Jesus gave unto me.

3. He laid his hand on me and heal'd me,
And bade me be every whit whole;
I touched but the hem of his garment,
And glory came thrilling my soul.

No. 151. Tune—O, TO BE NOTHING. Key C.

1. O, to be nothing, nothing,
Only to lie at his feet,
A broken and emptied vessel,
For the Master's use made meet,
Emptied that he might fill me
As forth to his service I go;
Broken, that so unhindered,
His life through me might flow.

2. O, to be nothing, nothing,
Only as led by his hand;
A messenger at his gateway,
Only waiting for his command;
Only an instrument ready
If is praises to sound at his will,
Willing, should he not require me
In silence to wait on him still.

3. O, to be nothing, nothing,
Painful the humbling may be:
Yet low in the dust I'd lay me
That the world might my Savior see,
Rather be nothing, nothing,—
To him let their voices be raised;
He is the Fountain of blessing,
He only is most to be praised.

No. 152. Tune—RETREAT. L. M. Key C.

1. Behold a stranger at the door!
He gently knocks, has knocked before,
Has waited long, is waiting still;
You treat no other friend so ill.

Cho.—Oh, let the dear Savior come in,
He'll cleanse thy heart from sin!
Oh, keep him no more out at the door,
But let the dear Savior come in.

2. Oh, lovely attitude!—he stands
With melting heart, and loaded hands.
Oh, matchless kindness!—and he shows
This matchless kindness to his foes!

3. But will he prove a friend indeed?
He will—the very friend you need;
The friend of sinners—yes, 'tis he,
With garments dyed on Calvary.

4. Rise, touched with gratitude divine,
Turn out his enemy and thine,
That soul-destroying monster, sin,—
And let the heavenly Stranger in.

No. 153. Tune—KNOCKING. Key E♭.

1. Knocking, knocking, who is there?
Waiting, waiting, oh, how fair!
'Tis a Pilgrim, strange and kingly,
Never such was seen before,
Ah! my soul, for such a wonder,
Wilt thou not undo the door?

2. Knocking, knocking, still He's there,
Waiting, waiting, wondrous fair;
But the door is hard to open,
For the weeds and ivy-vine,
With their dark and clinging tendrils,
Ever round the hinges twine.

3. Knocking, knocking—what, still there?
Waiting, waiting, grand and fair;
Yes, the pierced hand still knocketh,
And beneath the crowned hair
Beam the patient eyes, so tender,
Of thy Savior, waiting there.

No. 154. Tune—CHRISTMAS.
Key E♭.

1. In the cross of Christ I glory,
   Towering o'er the wrecks of time;
   All the light of sacred story
   Gathers round its head sublime.

2. When the woes of life o'ertake me,
   Hopes deceive, and fears annoy,
   Never shall the cross forsake me;
   Lo! it glows with peace and joy.

3. Bane and blessing, pain and pleasure,
   By the cross are sanctified:
   Peace is there, that knows no measure,
   Joys, that through all time abide.

—o—

No. 155. Tune—THE LORD WILL PROVIDE.
Key B♭.

1. In some way or other
   The Lord will provide;
   It may not be *my* way,
   It may not be *thy* way,
   And yet, in His *own* way,
   The Lord will provide.

CHO.—It may not be *my* way,
   It may not be *thy* way,
   And yet, in His *own* way,
   The Lord will provide.

2. At some time or other
   The Lord will provide;
   It may not be *my* time,
   It may not be *thy* time,
   And yet, in His *own* time,
   The Lord will provide.

3. Despond, then, no longer;
   The Lord will provide;
   And this be the token—
   No word he hath spoken
   Was ever yet broken,—
   The Lord will provide.

4. March on, then, right boldly;
   The sea shall divide;
   The pathway made glorious
   With shoutings victorious,
   We'll join in the chorus,
   The Lord will provide.

—o—

No. 156. Tune—TRUSTING.
Key G.

1. I am coming to the cross;
   I am poor, and weak, and blind;
   I am counting all but dross,
   I shall full salvation find.

CHO.—I am trusting, Lord, in Thee,
   Blest Lamb of Calvary;
   Humbly at Thy cross I bow,
   Save me, Jesus, save me now.

2. Long my heart has sighed for Thee,
   Long has evil reigned within;
   Jesus sweetly speaks to me,—
   "I will cleanse you from all sin."

3. Here I give my all to Thee,
   Friends, and time, and earthly store,
   Soul and body, Thine to be,—
   Wholly thine for evermore.

4. In thy promises I trust,
   Now I feel the blood applied;
   I am prostrate in the dust,
   I with Christ am crucified.

5. Jesus comes! He fills my soul!
   Perfected in Him I am;
   I am every whit made whole;
   Glory, glory to the Lamb.

—o—

No. 157. Tune—HOLY SPIRIT.
Key G.

1. Holy Spirit, faithful guide,
   Ever near the Christian's side;
   Gently lead us by the hand,
   Pilgrims in a desert land;
   Weary souls for e'er rejoice,
   While they hear that sweetest voice,
   Whisp'ring softly, wanderer come!
   Follow me, I'll guide thee home.

2. Ever present, truest Friend,
   Ever near Thine aid to lend,
   Leave us not to doubt and fear,
   Groping on in darkness drear,
   When the storms are raging sore,
   Hearts grow faint, and hopes give o'er,
   Whispering softly, wanderer come!
   Follow me, I'll guide thee home.

—o—

No. 158. Tune—COME TO JESUS.
Key F.

1. Come to Jesus, come to Jesus,
   Come to Jesus just now,
   Just now, come to Jesus,
   Come to Jesus, just now

2. He will save you, etc.
3. He is able, etc.
4. He is willing, etc
5. He is waiting, etc.
6. He will hear you, etc.
7. He will cleanse you, etc.
8. He'll renew you, etc.
9. He'll forgive you, etc.
10. If you trust Him, etc.
11. He will save you, etc.

No. 159. Tune—BOYLSTON. S. M. Key C.

1. Revive thy work, O Lord!
Thy mighty arm make bare; [dead,
Speak, with the voice that wakes the
And make Thy people hear.

2. Revive Thy work, O Lord!
Disturb this sleep of death;
Quicken the smouldering embers now
By Thine almighty breath.

3. Revive Thy work, O Lord!
Exalt Thy precious name;
And, by the Holy Ghost, our love,
For Thee and Thine inflame.

4. Revive Thy work, O Lord!
And give refreshing showers;
The glory shall be all Thine own,
The blessing, Lord, be ours.

—o—

No. 160. Tune—FOR YOU I AM PRAYING. Key A♭.

1. I have a Savior, He's pleading in
glory,
A dear, loving Savior, tho' earth's
friends be few;
And now He is watching in tenderness
o'er me,
And oh, that my Savior were your
Savior too.

CHO.—For you I am praying,
For you I am praying,
For you I am praying,
I'm praying for you.

2. I have a Father: to me He has given
A hope for eternity, blessed and true;
And soon will He call me to meet Him
in heaven,
But oh, that He'd let me bring you
with me too.

3. I have a robe: 'tis resplendent in
whiteness,
Awaiting in glory my wondering view;
Oh, when I receive it all shining in
brightness, [one too!
Dear friend, could I see you receiving

4. I have a peace: it is calm as a river—
A peace that the friends of this world
never knew,
My Savior alone is its Author and Giver,
And oh, could I know it was given to
you!

5. When Jesus has found you, tell others
the story, [too;
That my loving Savior is your Savior
Then pray that your Savior may bring
them to glory,
And prayer will be answered—'twas
answered for you.

No. 161. Tune—MERIBAH. C. P. M. Key E♭.

1. When Thou, my righteous Judge,
shalt come,
To bring Thy ransom'd people home
Shall I among them stand?
Shall such a worthless worm as I,
Who sometimes am afraid to die,
Be found at Thy right hand?

2. I love to meet among them now,
Before Thy gracious feet to bow,
Though vilest of them all;
But can I bear the piercing thought—
What if my name should be left out,
When Thou for them shalt call?

3. Prevent, prevent it by Thy grace;
Be Thou, dear Lord, my hiding-place,
In this the accepted day:
Thy pardoning voice, oh, let me hear!
To still my unbelieving fear;
Nor let me fall, I pray.

4. Let me among Thy saints be found,
Whene'er the archangel's trump shall
sound,
To see Thy smiling face;
Then loudest of the crowd I'll sing,
While heaven's resounding mansions
With shouts of sovereign grace. [ring

—o—

No. 162. Tune—JESUS PAID IT ALL. Key E♭.

1. I hear the Savior say,
Thy strength indeed is small;
Child of weakness, watch and pray,
Find in me thine all in all.

CHO.—Jesus paid it all,
All to Him I owe;
Sin had left a crimson stain:
He washed it white as snow.

2. Lord, now indeed I find
Thy power and Thine alone,
Can change the leper's spots,
And melt the heart of stone.

3. For nothing good have I
Whereby Thy grace to claim—
I'll wash my garment white
In the blood of Calvary's Lamb.

4. When from my dying bed
My ransomed soul shall rise,
Then "Jesus paid it all"
Shall rend the vaulted skies.

5. And when before the throne
I stand in Him complete,
I'll lay my trophies down,
All down at Jesus' feet.

No. 163. Tune—SOLID ROCK. Key A♯.

1. My hope is built on nothing less
Than Jesus' blood and righteousness;
I dare not trust the sweetest frame,
But wholly lean on Jesus' name.

Cho.—On Christ, the solid rock, I stand:
All other ground is sinking sand,
All other ground is sinking sand.

2. When darkness veils His lovely face,
I rest on His unchanging grace;
In every high and stormy gale,
My anchor holds within the vail.

3. His oath, His covenant, His blood,
Support me in the whelming flood;
When all around my soul gives way,
He then is all my hope and stay.

4. When He shall come with trumpet sound,
O, may I then in Him be found;
Drest in His righteousness alone,
Faultless to stand before the throne!

No. 164. Tune—BETHANY. Key G.

1. Savior! Thy dying love
Thou gavest me,
Nor should I aught withhold,
Dear Lord, from Thee;
In love my soul would bow,
My heart fulfill its vow,
Some offering bring Thee now,
Something for Thee.

2. At the blest mercy seat,
Pleading for me,
My feeble faith looks up,
Jesus to Thee:
Help me the cross to bear,
Thy wondrous love declare,
Some song to raise, or prayer,
Something for Thee!

3. Give me a faithful heart—
Likeness to Thee—
That each departing day
Henceforth may see
Some work of love begun,
Some deed of kindness done,
Some wand'rer sought and won,
Something for Thee.

4. All that I am and have—
Thy gifts so free—
In joy, in grief, through life,
Dear Lord, for Thee!
And when thy face I see,
My ransomed soul shall be
Through all eternity,
Something for Thee.

No. 165. Tune—I LEFT ALL WITH JESUS. Key G.

1. I left all with Jesus
Long ago;
All my sins I brought Him,
And my woe.
When by faith I saw Him
On the tree,
Heard His small, still whisper,
"'Tis for thee,'
‖: From my heart the burden
Rolled away—happy day! :‖

2. I leave it all with Jesus,
For he knows
How to steal the bitter
From life's woes;
How to gild the tear-drop
With his smile,
Make the desert garden
Bloom awhile;
‖: When my weakness leaneth
On His might, all seems light. :‖

3. I leave it all with Jesus
Day by day;
Faith can firmly trust Him,
Come what may.
Hope has dropped her anchor,
Found her rest
In the calm, sure haven
Of His breast;
‖: Love esteems it heaven
To abide at His side. :‖

4. Oh, leave it *all* with Jesus,
Drooping soul!
Tell not *half* thy story,
But the whole.
Worlds on worlds are hanging
On his hand,
Life and death are waiting
His command.

No. 166. Tune—FADE EACH EARTHLY JOY. Key A♭.

1. Fade, fade each earthly joy,
Jesus is mine!
Break every tender tie,
Jesus is mine!
Dark is the wilderness,
Earth has no resting place,
Jesus alone can bless,
Jesus is mine!

2. Tempt not my soul away,
Jesus is mine!
Here would I ever stay,
Jesus is mine!
Perishing things of clay,
Born but for one brief day,
Pass from my heart away,
Jesus is mine!

3. Farewell, ye dreams of night,
   Jesus is mine!
Lost in this dawning light
   Jesus is mine!
All that my soul has tried,
Left but a dismal void,
Jesus has satisfied,
   Jesus is mine!

4. Farewell, mortality,
   Jesus is mine!
Welcome eternity,
   Jesus is mine!
Welcome, O loved and blest,
Welcome, sweet scenes of rest,
Welcome, my Savior's breast,
   Jesus is mine!

—o—

No. 167. Tune—SAVIOR LEAD US.
Key B♭.

1. Savior, like a shepherd lead us,
   Much we need Thy tend'rest care;
In thy pleasant pastures feed us,
For our use Thy folds prepare.
‖: Blessed Jesus, Blessed Jesus,
Thou hast bought us, Thine we are.:‖

2. We are Thine, do Thou befriend us,
   Be the Guardian of our way;
Keep Thy flock, from sin defend us,
Seek us when we go astray.
   Blessed Jesus,
Hear, O hear us, when we pray.

3. Thou hast promised to receive us,
   Poor and sinful though we be,
Thou hast mercy to relieve us,
Grace to cleanse, and power to free.
   Blessed Jesus,
We will early turn to Thee.

4. Early let us seek Thy favor,
   Early let us do Thy will;
Blessed Lord and only Savior,
With Thy love our bosoms fill.
   Blessed Jesus,
Thou hast loved us, love us still.

—o—

No. 168. Tune—WEBB. 7s & 6s.
Key B♭.

1. Stand up! stand up for Jesus!
   Ye soldiers of the cross;
Lift high His royal banner,
   It must not suffer loss;
From victory unto victory
   His army He shall lead,
Till every foe is vanquished,
   And Christ is Lord indeed.

2. Stand up! stand up for Jesus!
   Stand in His strength alone;
The arm of flesh will fail you—
   Ye dare not trust your own;
Put on the gospel armor,
   And, watching unto prayer,
Where duty calls, or danger,
   Be never wanting there.

3. Stand up! stand up for Jesus!
   The strife will not be long;
This day the noise of battle,
   The next, the victor's song;
To him that overcometh,
   A crown of life shall be;
He with the King of Glory
   Shall reign eternally.

—o—

No. 169. Tune—SIMPLY TRUSTING.
Key A♭.

1. Simply trusting every day,
Trusting thro' a stormy way;
Even when my faith is small,
Trusting Jesus, that is all.

CHO.—Trusting as the moments fly,
Trusting as the days go by;
Trusting Him whate'er befall,
Trusting Jesus, that is all.

2. Brightly doth His Spirit shine
Into this poor heart of mine;
While He leads I can not fall,
Trusting Jesus, that is all.

3. Singing, if my way is clear;
Praying, if the path is drear;
If in danger, for Him call;
Trusting Jesus, that is all.

4. Trusting Him while life shall last,
Trusting Him till earth is past;
Till within the jasper wall,
Trusting Jesus, that is all.

—o—

No. 170. Tune—SWEET HOME.
Key E♭.

1. O eyes that are weary, and hearts that
   are sore, [more;
Look off unto Jesus, and sorrow no
The light of His countenance shineth so
   bright, [be no night.
That on earth, as in heaven, there need

2. "Looking off unto Jesus," my eyes
   can not see, [around me:
The troubles and dangers that throng
They can not be blinded with sorrowful
   tears, [fears.
They can not be shadowed with unbelief-

3. "Looking off unto Jesus," I go not
   astray; [the way;
My eyes are on Him, and He shows me
The path may seem dark, as He leads me
   along,
But following Jesus, I can not go wrong.

4. "Looking off unto Jesus," my heart
   can not fear, [near;
Its trembling is still when I see Jesus
I know that His power my safeguard
   will be,
"For why are ye troubled?" he saith
   unto me.

No. 171. Tune—TURN TO THE LORD. Key G.

1. Come, ye sinners, poor and needy,
Weak and wounded, sick and sore,
Jesus ready stands to save you,
Full of pity, love and power,
‖: He is able, He is able,
He is willing, doubt no more. :‖

2. Come, ye thirsty, come and welcome;
God's free bounty glorify;
True belief and true repentance,
Every grace that brings us nigh—
‖: Without money, without money,
Come to Jesus Christ and buy. :‖

3. Come, ye weary, heavy laden,
Lost and ruined by the fall;
If you tarry till you're better,
You will never come at all:
‖: Not the righteous—not the righteous,
Sinners, Jesus came to call. :‖

4. Let not conscience make you linger,
Nor of fitness fondly dream;
All the fitness He requireth,
Is to feel your need of Him:
‖: This He gives you—this He gives you,
'Tis the Spirit's rising beam. :‖

No. 172. Tune—RETREAT. L. M. Key E♭.

1. From every stormy wind that blows,
From every swelling tide of woes,
There is a calm, a sure retreat,
'Tis found beneath the mercy-seat.

2. There is a place where Jesus sheds
The oil of gladness on our heads;
A place than all besides more sweet,
It is the blood-bought mercy-seat.

3. There is a scene where spirits blend,
Where friend holds fellowship with friend,
Though sundered far, by faith they meet
Around one common mercy-seat.

No. 173. Tune—"REVIVE US AGAIN." Key G.

1. We praise Thee, O God! for the Son of Thy love,
For Jesus who died, and is now gone above!

Cho.—Hallelujah! thine the glory, Hallelujah! Amen,
Hallelujah! thine the glory, revive us again.

2. We praise Thee, O God! for thy Spirit of light,
Who has shown us our Savior, and scattered our night.

3. All glory and praise to the Lamb that was slain,
Who has borne all our sins, and cleansed every stain.

4. All glory and praise to the God of all grace,
Who has bought us, and sought us, and guided our ways.

5. Revive us again; fill each heart with Thy love;
May each soul be rekindled with fire from above.

No. 174. Tune—JUDGMENT HYMN. Key D.

1. The judgment day is coming, coming,
The judgment day is coming; [coming,
O that great day!

Cho.—Let us take the wings of the morn-
And fly away to Jesus; [ing,
Let us take the wings of the morning,
And sound the jubilee.

2. I heard the trumpet sounding, sounding, sounding,
I heard the trumpet sounding,
On that great day.

3. I saw the Judge descending, descending, descending,
I saw the Judge descending,
On that great day.

4. I saw the dead arising, arising, arising,
I saw the dead arising,
On that great day.

5. I heard the thunder rolling, rolling,
I heard the thunder rolling, [rolling,
On that great day.

6. I saw the lightning blazing, blazing,
I saw the lightning blazing, [blazing,
On that great day.

7. I heard the wicked wailing, wailing,
I heard the wicked wailing, [wailing,
On that great day.

Cho.—For they took not the wings of the morning,
Nor flew away to Jesus; [morning,
For they took not the wings of the
Nor sang the jubilee.

8. I heard the righteous shouting, shouting, shouting,
I heard the righteous shouting,
On that great day.

Cho.—For they took the wings of the
And flew away to Jesus; [morning,
For they took the wings of the morning,
And sang the jubilee.

No. 175. Tune—HEBRON. L. M. Key B♭.

1. While life prolongs its precious light,
Mercy is found, and peace is given;
But soon, ah, soon, approaching night
Shall blot out every hope of heaven.

2. While God invites, how blest the day!
How sweet the Gospel's charming sound!
Come, sinners, haste, O haste away,
While yet a pard'ning God is found.

3. Soon, borne on time's most rapid wing,
Shall death command you to the grave,
Before His bar your spirits bring,
And none be found to hear or save.

4. In that lone land of deep despair,
No Sabbath's heavenly light shall rise,—
No God regard your bitter prayer,
No Savior call you to the skies.

5. Now God invites; how blest the day!
How sweet the Gospel's charming sound!
Come, sinners, haste, O haste away,
While yet a pard'ning God is found.

—o—

No. 176. Tune—LABAN. S. M. Key D.

1. I love Thy kingdom, Lord,
The house of Thine abode,
The Church our blest Redeemer saved
With His own precious blood.

2. I love Thy Church, O God!
Her walls before thee stand,
Dear as the apple of thine eye,
And graven on Thy hand.

3. For her my tears sha'l fall;
For her my prayers ascend;
To her my cares and toils be given,
Till toils and cares shall end.

4. Beyond my highest joy
I prize her heavenly ways;
Her sweet communion, solemn vows,
Her hymns of love and praise.

5. Sure as Thy truth shall last,
To Zion shall be given
The brightest glories earth can yield,
And brighter bliss of heaven.

—o—

No. 177. Tune—NOTHING BUT LEAVES. Key E♭.

1. Nothing but leaves, the spirit grieves
O'er years of wasted life!
O'er sins indulged while conscience slept,
O'er vows and promises unkept,
And reap from years of strife—
Nothing but leaves! nothing but leaves!

2. Nothing but leaves! No gathered sheaves
Of life's fair ripening grain;
We sow our seeds: lo! tares and weeds—
Words, idle words, for earnest deeds—
Then reap, with toil and pain,
Nothing but leaves! nothing but leaves!

3. Nothing but leaves! Sad mem'ry weaves
No vail to hide the past,
And as we trace our weary way,
And count each lost and misspent day,
We sadly find at last—
Nothing but leaves! nothing but leaves!

4. Ah, who shall thus the Master meet,
And bring but withered leaves?
Ah, who shall at the Savior's feet,
Before the awful judgment-seat
Lay down for golden sheaves,
Nothing but leaves! nothing but leaves!

—o—

No. 178. Tune—HENDON. 7s. Key G.

1. Come, my soul, thy suit prepare,
Jesus loves to answer prayer,
He Himself has bid thee pray,
Therefore will not say thee nay.

2. Thou art coming to a King,
Large petitions with thee bring,
For His grace and power are such,
None can ever ask too much.

3. With my burden I begin,
Lord, remove this load of sin;
Let Thy blood for sinners spilt,
Set my conscience free from guilt.

4. Lord, I come to Thee for rest,
Take possession of my breast,
There Thy blood-bought right maintain,
And without a rival reign.

—o—

No. 179. Tune—HAMBURG. L. M. Key F.

1. 'Tis midnight; and on Olive's brow,
The star is dimm'd that lately shone;
'Tis midnight; in the garden now
The suff'ring Savior prays alone.

2. 'Tis midnight; and from all removed,
The Savior wrestles lone with fears;
E'en that disciple whom He loved
Heeds not his Master's grief and tears.

3. 'Tis midnight; and for others' guilt,
The Man of Sorrow weeps in blood;
Yet He, who hath in anguish knelt,
Is not forsaken by His God.

4. 'Tis midnight; and, from ether-plains
Is born the song that angels know;
Unheard by mortals are the strains
That sweetly soothe the Savior's woe.

‖:Will any one then at the beautiful gate,
Be waiting and watching for me?:‖

Cho.—‖:Be waiting and watching,
Be waiting and watching for me?:‖

2. There are little ones glancing about in my path,
In want of a friend and a guide;
There are dear little eyes looking up into mine,
Whose tears might be easily dried.
But Jesus may beckon the children away [glee—
In the midst of their grief and their
‖:Will any of them, at the beautiful gate,
Be waiting and watching for me?:‖

3. There are old and forsaken who linger awhile
In homes which their dearest have left; [love
And a few gentle words or an action of
May cheer their sad spirits bereft,
But the Reaper is near to the long standing corn
The weary will soon be set free—
‖:Will any of them, at the beautiful gate,
Be waiting and watching for me?:‖

4. Oh, should I be brought there by the bountiful grace
Of Him who delights to forgive,
Though I bless not the weary about in my path,
Pray only for self while I live,—
Methinks I should mourn o'er my sinful neglect,
If sorrow in heaven can be, [gate,
‖:Should no one I love, at the beautiful
Be waiting and watching for me!:‖

—o—

No. 181. Tune—WATCHMAN. 8s & 7s. Key G.

1. Watchman, tell me does the morning
Of fair Zion's glory dawn;
Have the signs that mark his coming,
Yet upon my pathway shone?
Pilgrim, yes, arise, look round thee,
Light is breaking in the skies;
Spurn the unbelief that bound thee,
Morning dawns, arise, arise!

No. 182. THOUGHT. Key B♭.

1. One sweetly solemn thought
Comes to me o'er and o'er,
I'm nearer home to-day, to-day,
Than I have been before.

Cho.—Nearer my home, nearer my home,
Nearer my home to-day, to-day,
Than I have been before.

2. Nearer my Father's house
Where many mansions be;
Nearer the great white throne to-day,
Nearer the crystal sea.

3. Nearer the bound of life
Where the burdens are laid down;
Nearer to leave the cross to-day,
And nearer to the crown.

4. Be near me when my feet
Are slipping o'er the brink;
For I am nearer home to-day,
Perhaps, than now I think.

—o—

No. 183. Tune—IN THE SILENT MIDNIGHT WATCHES. Key F.

1. In the silent midnight watches,
List—thy bosom's door!
How it knocketh, knocketh, knocketh,
Knocketh evermore!
Say not 'tis thy pulse's beating,
'Tis my heart of sin;
'Tis thy Savior knocks, and crieth,
"Rise, and let me in!"

2. Death comes down with reckless foot-
To the hall and hut; [steps,
Think you death will tarry knocking,
When the door is shut?
Jesus waiteth, waiteth, waiteth;
But the door is fast;
Grieved, away thy Savior goeth,
Death breaks in at last.

3. Then 'tis time to stand entreating
Christ to let thee in;
At the gate of heaven beating,
Wailing for thy sin;
Nay! alas, thou guilty creature!
Hast thou, then, forgot?
Jesus waited long to know thee,
Now He knows thee not.

No. 184. Tune—EXPOSTULATION. 11s. Key A♭.

1. Oh, turn ye, oh, turn ye, for why will
    ye die, [nigh?
When God in great mercy is coming so
Now Jesus invites you, the Spirit says,
    "Come," [home.
And angels are waiting to welcome you

2. How vain the delusion, that while
    you delay, [melt away;
Your hearts may grow better, your chains
Come guilty, come wretched, come just
    as you are,
All helpless and dying to Jesus repair.

3. The contrite in heart He will freely
    receive. [believe?
Oh! why will you not the glad message
If sin be your burden, why will you not
    come? [you come home.
'Tis you He makes welcome; He bids

—o—

No. 185. Tune—CALLING US AWAY. Key B♭.

1. Give me the wings of faith to rise,
    Within the vail, and see
The saints above, how great their joys,
    How bright their glories be.

CHO.—Many are the friends who are
        waiting to-day
    Happy on the golden strand,
Many are the voices calling us away,
    To join their glorious band:
‖: Calling us away, calling us away,
    Calling to the better land. :‖

2. Once they were mourners here below,
    And pour'd out cries and tears;
They wrestled hard, as we do now,
    With sins, and doubts and fears.

3. I ask them whence their victory
    They, with united breath, [came:
Ascribe their conquest to the Lamb,
    Their triumph to His death.

—o—

No. 186. Tune—JESUS DIED FOR ME. Key E♭.

1. Alas! and did my Savior bleed?
    And did my Sovereign die?
Would He devote that sacred head
    For such a worm as I?

CHO.—Jesus died for you,
        Jesus died for me,
    Yes, Jesus died for all mankind,
        Bless God salvation's free.

2. Was it for crimes that I had done
    He groaned upon the tree?
Amazing pity! grace unknown!
    And love beyond degree.

3. Well might the sun in darkness hide,
    And shut his glories in,
When Christ the mighty Maker died
    For man the creature's sin.

4. Thus might I hide my blushing face
    While His dear cross appears,
Dissolve my heart in thankfulness,
    And melt mine eyes to tears.

5. But drops of grief can ne'er repay
    The debt of love I owe;
Here, Lord, I give myself away;
    'Tis all that I can do.

—o—

No. 187. Tune—ST. MARTINS. C. M. Key G.

1. All that I was, my sin, my guilt,
    My death, was all my own:
All that I am I owe to Thee,
    My gracious God, alone.

2. The evil of my former state
    Was mine, and only mine;
The good in which I now rejoice
    Is Thine and only Thine.

3. The darkness of my former state,
    The bondage,—all was mine,
The light of life in which I walk,
    The liberty,—is Thine.

4. Thy grace first made me feel my sin,
    And taught me to believe;
Then, in believing, peace I found,
    And now in Thee I live.

5. All that I am e'en here on earth,
    All that I hope to be—
When Jesus comes and glory dawns,
    I owe it, Lord, to Thee.

—o—

No. 188. Tune—O, HOW HAPPY.

1. O, how happy are they
    Who their Savior obey,
And have laid up their treasure above!
    Tongue can never express
    The sweet comfort and peace
Of a soul in its earliest love.

2. That sweet comfort was mine,
    When the favor divine
I first found in the blood of the Lamb;
    When my heart first believed,
    What a joy I received,
What a heaven in Jesus' name!

3. 'Twas a heaven below,
    My Redeemer to know:
And the angels could do nothing more
    Than to fall at his feet,
    And the story repeat,
And the Lover of sinners adore.

No. 189. Tune—GARDEN HYMN. Key E.

1. The Lord into His garden comes,
The spices yield their rich perfumes,
‖: The lilies grow and thrive ; :‖
Refreshing show'rs of grace divine
From Jesus flow to every vine,
‖: Which makes the dead revive. :‖

2. This makes the dry and barren ground
In springs of water to abound,
‖: And fruitful soil become ; :‖
The desert blossoms as the rose,
When Jesus conquers all His foes,
‖: And makes His people one. :‖

3. The glorious time is rolling on,
The gracious work is now begun,
‖: My soul a witness is, :‖
Come, taste and see the pardon free,
For all mankind as well as me ;
‖: Who comes to Christ may live. :‖

4. The worst of sinners here may find
A Savior pitiful and kind,
‖: Who will them all relieve ; :‖
None are too late if they repent ;
Out of one sinner legions went,
‖: Jesus did him receive. :‖

5. We feel that heaven is now begun,
It issues from the sparkling throne,
‖: From Jesus' throne on high :‖
It comes in floods we can't contain,
We drink, and drink, and drink again,
‖: And yet we still are dry. ;‖

6. But when we come to dwell above,
And all surround the throne of love,
‖: We'll drink a full supply ; :‖
Jesus will lead His armies through,
To living fountains where they flow,
‖: That never will run dry. :‖

7. There we shall reign, and shout, and sing,
And make the upper regions ring,
‖: When all the saints get home ; :‖
Come on, come on, my brethren dear,
Soon we shall meet together there,
‖: For Jesus bids us come. :‖

8. Amen, amen, my soul replies,
I'm bound to meet you in the skies,
‖: And claim my mansion there :‖
Now here's my heart and here's my hand,
To meet you in that heavenly land,
‖: Where we shall part no more. :‖

—o—

No. 190. Tune—WELTON. L. M. Key B♭.

1. Blest hour! when God himself draws nigh,
Well pleased His people's voice to hear,
To hush the penitential sigh,
And wipe away the mourner's tear.

2. Blest hour! for where the Lord resorts,
Foretastes of future bliss are given,
And mortals find His earthly courts
The house of God, the gate of heaven.

3. Hail, peaceful hour! supremely blest,
Amid the hours of worldly care;
The hour that yields the Spirit rest,
That sacred hour—the hour of prayer.

4. And when my hours of prayer are past,
And this frail tenement decays,
Then may I spend in heaven at last
A never-ending hour of praise.

—o—

No. 191. Tune—LABAN. S. M. Key D.

1. O Lord, Thy work revive
In Zion's gloomy hour,
And let our dying graces live,
By thy restoring power.

2. Oh, let Thy chosen few
Awake to earnest prayer;
Their sacred vows again renew,
And walk in filial fear.

3. Thy Spirit then will speak
Through lips of feeble clay,
Till hearts of adamant shall break,
Till rebels shall obey.

4. Now lend thy gracious ear;
Now listen to our cry;
Oh, come and bring salvation near;
Our souls on thee rely.

—o—

No. 192. Tune—CROSS AND CROWN. Key B♭.

1. Must Jesus bear the cross alone,
And all the world go free ?
No: there's a cross for every one,
And there's a cross for me.

2. How happy are the saints above
Who once went sorrowing here;
But now they taste unmingled love,
And joy without a tear.

3. The consecrated cross I'll bear,
Till death shall set me free,
And then go home my crown to wear,—
For there's a crown for me!

4. O precious cross! O glorious crown!
O resurrection day!
Ye angels! from the stars flash down,
And bear my soul away.

No. 193. Tune—CORONATION. Key G.

1. O for a thousand tongues to sing
My great Redeemer's praise;
The glories of my God and King,
The triumph's of His grace.

2. My gracious Master and my God,
Assist me to proclaim,—
To spread through all the earth abroad,
The honors of Thy Name.

3. Jesus!—the name that charms our fears,
That bids our sorrows cease;
'Tis music to the sinner's ears,
'Tis life, and health, and peace.

4. He breaks the power of cancell'd sin,
He sets the pris'ner free;
His blood can make the foulest clean;
His blood avail'd for me.

—o—

No. 194. Tune—HENDON. 7s. Key G.

1. Jesus is gone up on high;
But His promise still is here,
"I will all your wants supply;
I will send the Comforter."

2. Let us now His promise plead,
Let us to His throne draw nigh;
Jesus knows His people's need;
Jesus hears His people's cry.

3. Send us, Lord, the Comforter,
Pledge and witness of Thy love,
Dwelling with Thy people here,
Leading them to joys above.

4. Till we reach the promised rest,
Till Thy face unveil'd we see,
Of this blessed hope possess'd,
Teach us, Lord, to live in Thee.

—o—

No. 195. Tune—"WILL YOU GO?" Key G.

1. We're traveling home to heaven above;
Will you go? Will you go?
To sing the Savior's dying love;
Will you go? Will you go?
Millions have reached that blest abode,
Anointed kings and priests of God;
And millions more are on the road;
Will you go? Will you go?

2. We're going to walk the planes of light;
Will you go? Will you go?
Far, far from curse and death and night;
Will you go? Will you go?
The crown of life we then shall wear,
The conqueror's palm we then shall bear,
And all the joys of heaven we'll share;
Will you go? Will you go?

3. The way to heaven is straight and plain;
Will you go? Will you go?
Repent, believe, be born again:
Will you go? Will you go?
The Savior cries aloud to thee,
"Take up thy cross and follow me,
And thou shalt my salvation see."
Will you go? Will you go?

—o—

No. 196. Tune—UXBRIDGE. L. M. Key F.

1. Jesus, assembled in Thy name,
This promise at Thy hand we claim;
We do believe, oh let us see [Thee,
Great signs and wonders wrought by

2. Command, and these dead souls shall live,
These blind at once their sight receive;
Speak, and these deaf shall hear Thy voice,
These dumb in loudest songs rejoice.

3. Now let Thy mighty power be known;
Now break or melt these hearts of stone:
We *do* believe, shall we not see [Thee?
New signs and wonders wrought by

4. Claim now the souls whom Thou hast bought; [sought;
Fetch home the wanderers Thou hast
See, Lord, we bring our wants to Thee;
Let this the hour of mercy be.

—o—

No. 197. Tune—SWEET HOUR OF PRAYER. Key D.

1. Sweet hour of prayer! sweet hour of prayer!
That calls me from a world of care,
And bids me at my Father's throne,
Make all my wants and wishes known;
In seasons of distress and grief,
My soul has often found relief,
‖: And oft escaped the tempter's snare
By thy return, sweet hour of prayer. :‖

2. Sweet hour of prayer! sweet hour of prayer!
Thy wings shall my petition bear
To Him whose truth and faithfulness
Engage the waiting soul to bless.
And since He bids me seek His face,
Believe His word, and trust His grace,
‖: I'll cast on Him my every care,
And wait for thee, sweet hour of prayer. :‖

3. Sweet hour of prayer! sweet hour of prayer!
May I thy consolation share:
Till, from Mount Pisgah's lofty height
I view my home and take my flight;
This robe of flesh I'll drop and rise
To seize the everlasting prize; [air,
‖: And shout, while passing through the
Farewell, farewell, sweet hour of prayer. :‖

No. 198. Tune—"LIFE IN A LOOK."
Key G.

1. There is life in a look at the crucified One,
There is life at this moment for thee;
Then look, sinners, look unto Him and be saved,
Unto Him who was nailed to the tree.

REF.—Look! look! look and live!
There is life in a look at the crucified One,
There is life at this moment for thee.

2. Oh, why was He there as the bearer of sin,
If on Jesus thy guilt was not laid?
Oh, why from His side flowed the sin-cleansing blood,
If His dying thy debt has not paid?

3. It is not thy tears of repentance and prayers,
But the blood that atones for the soul;
On Him, then, who shed it, thou mayest at once
Thy weight of iniquities roll.

4. Then doubt not thy welcome, since God has declared
There remained no more to be done;
That once in the end of the world he appeared,
And completed the work he begun.

5. Then take with rejoicing from Jesus at once
The life everlasting he gives;
And know with assurance thou never canst die
Since Jesus, thy righteousness, lives.

No. 199. Tune—HEBRON. L. M.
Key B♭.

1. While life prolongs its precious light,
Mercy is found, and peace is given;
But soon, ah, soon, approaching night
Shall blot out every hope of heaven.

2. While God invites, how blest the day!
How sweet the gospel's charming sound!
Come, sinners, haste, O haste away,
While yet a pard'ning God is found.

3. Soon, borne on time's most rapid wing,
Shall death command you to the grave,
Before His bar your spirits bring,
And none be found to hear or save.

4. In that lone land of deep despair,
No Sabbath's heavenly light shall rise,
No God regard your bitter prayer,
No Savior call you to the skies.

5. Now God invites; how blest the day!
How sweet the gospel's charming sound!
Come, sinners, haste, O haste away,
While yet a pard'ning God is found.

No. 200. Tune—SUN OF MY SOUL.
Key F.

1. Sun of my soul, Thou Savior dear,
It is not night if Thou be near;
Oh, may no earth-born cloud arise,
To hide Thee from Thy servant's eyes.

2. When the soft dews of kindly sleep,
My weary eyelids gently steep,
Be my last thought, how sweet to rest
Forever on my Savior's breast.

3. Abide with me from morn till eve,
For without Thee I can not live;
Abide with me when night is nigh,
For without Thee I dare not die.

4. If some poor wandering child of Thine
Have spurned to-day the voice Divine—
Now, Lord, the gracious work begin;
Let him no more lie down in sin.

5. Watch by the sick; enrich the poor
With blessings from Thy boundless store;
Be every mourner's sleep to-night,
Like infant's slumbers, pure and light.

6. Come near and bless us when we wake,
Ere through the world our way we take,
Till in the ocean of Thy love
We lose ourselves in heaven above.

No. 201. Tune—"MIGHTY LOVE."
Key C.

1. Oh, bliss of the purified, bliss of the free, [me;
I plunge in the crimson tide opened for
O'er sin and uncleanness exulting I stand, [His hand.
And point to the print of the nails in

CHO.—Oh, sing of His mighty love,
Sing of His mighty love,
Sing of His mighty love,
Mighty to save.

2. Oh, bliss of the purified, Jesus is mine, [pine;
No longer in dread condemnation I
In conscious salvation I sing of His grace, [face.
Who lifteth upon me the light of His

3. Oh, bliss of the purified! bliss of the pure! [can not cure;
No wound hath the soul that his blood
No sorrow-bowed head but may sweetly find rest, [breast.
No tears but may dry them on Jesus'

4 O Jesus, the crucified! Thee will I sing,
My blessed Redeemer, my God and my King; [o'er the grave,
My soul filled with rapture shall shout
And triumph in death in the "Mighty to Save."

No. 202. Tune—"OH! TO BE READY." Key B♭.

"Oh! to be ready, ready,"
  Ready to work or to rest,
Just as the Master wishes,
  Just as he thinks for the best;
Oh, to be ready, ready,
  Ready to go or to stay,
Just as the Master chooses,
  Just as He opens the way.

Cho.—Oh, to be ready, ready,
  Ready and watching in prayer,
Ready for Christ's appearing,
  Ready His glory to share.

2. Oh! to be ready, ready,
  Ready God's word to obey;
Shunning the path of danger,
  Seeking the one narrow way.
Oh! to be ready, ready,
  Ready to suffer His will,
Whom the Lord loves He chastens,
  Chastens for good, not for ill.

3. Oh! to be ready, ready,
  Ready to go at His call,
Over the cold, dark river,
  Flowing so near to us all.
Oh! to be ready, ready,
  Ready my dear ones to meet,
Shouting the Savior's praises,
  Casting their crowns at His feet.

—o—

No. 203. Tune—TAKE ME AS I AM. Key A♭.

1. Jesus, my Lord, to thee I cry,
Unless thou help me I must die;
Oh, bring thy free salvation nigh
And take me as I am!

Ref.—Take me as I am,
  Take me as I am;
Oh, bring thy free salvation nigh,
  And take me as I am.

2. Helpless I am, and full of guilt,
But yet for me thy blood was spilt,
And thou can'st make me what thou wilt,
But take me as I am!

3. No preparation can I make,
My best resolves I only break,
Yet save me for thine own name's sake,
And take me as I am!

4. I thirst, I long to know thy love,
Thy full salvation I would prove;
But since to thee I can not move,
Oh, take me as I am!

5. If thou hast work for me to do,
Inspire my will, my heart renew,
And work both in and by me too,
But take me as I am!

6. And when at last the work is done,
The battle o'er, the vict'ry won,
Still, still my cry shall be alone,
  Lord, take me as I am!

No. 204. Tune—"DENNIS." Key F.

1. Did Christ o'er sinners weep,
  And shall our cheeks be dry?
Let floods of penitential grief
  Burst forth from every eye.

2. The Son of God in tears
  The wond'ring angels see;
Be thou astonish'd, O my soul;
  He shed those tears for thee.

3. He wept that we might weep;
  Each sin demands a tear;
In heaven alone no sin is found,
  And there's no weeping there.

—o—

No. 205. Tune—"ARLINGTON." Key B♭.

1. How sweet, how heavenly is the sight,
  When those who love the Lord
In one another's peace delight,
  And thus fulfill his word.

2. When each can feel his brother's sigh,
  And with him bear a part;
When sorrow flows from eye to eye,
  And joy from heart to heart.

3. When, free from envy, scorn and pride,
  Our wishes all above,
Each can his brother's failings hide,
  And show a brother's love.

4. Let love, in one delightful stream,
  Through every bosom flow;
And union sweet and dear esteem
  In every action glow.

—o—

No. 206. Tune—WOODWORTH. L. M. Key B♭.

1. Just as I am, without one plea
But that thy blood was shed for me,
And that thou bidd'st me to come to thee,
O Lamb of God! I come, I come!

2. Just as I am, and waiting not
To rid my soul of one dark blot,
To thee, whose blood can cleanse each spot,
O Lamb of God! I come, I come!

3. Just as I am, though tossed about,
With many a conflict, many a doubt,
Fightings and fears within, without,
O Lamb of God! I come, I come!

4. Just as I am, poor, wretched, blind,
Sight, riches, healing of the mind,
Yea, all I need, in thee to find,
O Lamb of God! I come, I come!

5. Just as I am, thou wilt receive,
Wilt welcome, pardon, cleanse, relieve;
Because thy promise I believe,
O Lamb of God! I come, I come!

No. 207. Tune—"OH! HOW HE LOVES."
Key D.

1. One there is above all others,
   Oh, how He loves!
His is love beyond a brother's,
   Oh, how He loves!
Earthly friends may fail or leave us,
One day soothe, the next day grieve us;
But this Friend will ne'er deceive us,
   Oh, how He loves!

2. 'Tis eternal love to know Him,
   Oh, how He loves!
Think, oh, think how much we owe Him,
   Oh, how He loves!
With His precious blood He bought us;
In the wilderness He sought us,
To His fold He safely brought us,
   Oh, how He loves!

3. Blessed Jesus! would you know Him,
   Oh, how He loves!
Give yourself entirely to Him,
   Oh, how He loves!
Think no longer of the morrow,
From the past new courage borrow,
Jesus carries all your sorrow,
   Oh, how He loves!

4. All your sins shall be forgiven,
   Oh, how He loves!
Backward shall your foes be driven,
   Oh, how He loves!
Best of blessings He'll provide you,
Nought but good shall e'er betide you,
Safe to glory He will guide you,
   Oh, how He loves!

—o—

No. 208. Tune—DELIVERANCE WILL COME.
Key F.

1. I saw a way-worn trav'ler,
   In tatter'd garments clad,
And struggling up the mountain,
   It seemed that he was sad;
His back was laden heavy,
   His strength was almost gone,
Yet he shouted as he journeyed,
   Deliverance will come!

Cho.—Then palms of victory, crowns of
   glory,
   Palms of victory I shall wear.

2. The summer sun was shining,
   The sweat was on his brow,
His garments worn and dusty,
   His step seemed very slow:
But he kept pressing onward,
   For he was wending home;
Still shouting as he journeyed,
   Deliverance will come!

3. The songsters in the arbor
   That stood beside the way
Attracted his attention,
   Inviting his delay:
His watchword being "Onward!"
   He stopped his ears and ran,
Still shouting as he journeyed,
   Deliverance will come!

4. I saw him in the evening,
   The sun was bending low,
He'd overtopped the mountain,
   And reached the vale below:
He saw the golden city,—
   His everlasting home,—
And shouted loud, Hosanna,
   Deliverance will come!

5. While gazing on that city,
   Just o'er the narrow flood,
A band of holy angels
   Came from the throne of God,
They bore him on their pinions
   Safe o'er the dashing foam;
And joined him in his triumph,—
   Deliverance has come!

6. I heard the song of triumph
   They sang upon that shore,
Saying, Jesus has redeemed us
   To suffer nevermore:
Then, casting his eyes backward
   On the race which he had run,
He shouted loud, Hosanna,
   Deliverance has come!

—o—

No. 209. Tune—NOT KNOWING.
Music on page 74.

1. For perhaps the dreaded future
   Is less bitter than I think;
The Lord may sweeten the waters
   Before I stoop to drink;
Or, if Marah must be Marah,
   He will stand beside its brink.

2. It may be He keeps waiting
   Till the coming of my feet,
Some gift of such rare blessedness,
   Some joy so strangely sweet,
That my lips shall only tremble,
   With the thanks they can not speak.

3. O restful, blissful ignorance!
   'Tis blessed not to know,
It stills me in those mighty arms
   Which will not let me go,
And hushes my soul to rest
   On the bosom which loves me so!

4. My heart shrinks back from trials
   Which the future may disclose,
Yet I never had a sorrow
   But what the dear Lord chose;
So I send the coming tears back,
   With the whispered word, "He knows."

INDEX.

[Titles in SMALL CAPITALS; First lines in Roman.]

Title / First line	No.
ABIDING TRUST	5
ABUNDANTLY ABLE TO SAVE	10
Art thou weary with transgression	29
As clay in the hands of the potter	59
ALMOST	94
ART THOU WEARY, ART THOU LANGUID?	108
Am I a soldier of the cross?	122
All hail the power of Jesus' name	125
Arise, my soul, arise	140
Alas! and did my Savior bleed	186
All that I was, my sin, my guilt	187
Believe on the Lord	5
Before my face	38
BEHOLD HIS OFFERED SALVATION	46
BETHESDA IS OPEN FOR THEE	49
BLESSED ASSURANCE	82
BRINGING IN THE SHEAVES	90
BREAK THIS HEART OF MINE	109
Before I strive to save poor souls	109
BEHOLD ME STANDING AT THE DOOR	111
Behold a stranger at the door	152
Blest hour, when God himself draws nigh	190
Blest be the tie that binds	123
COME AND BE BLEST	14
COME, SINNER, COME	19
COME AND SEE	21
COME UNTO ME	25
Come, weary souls	25
COME TO JESUS	29
Come, poor sinners	33
COME, GREAT DELIVERER, COME	51
Come, trembling soul	56
CLEFT FOR ME	77
Come, dear Savior	85
COME, YE DISCONSOLATE	98
COME TO THE CROSS	115
Come, thou fount of every blessing	144
Come to Jesus	158
Come, ye sinners, poor and needy	171
Come, my soul, thy suit prepare	178
DRAW ME NEARER	26
Deep and grand in tones sublime	73
Dear Jesus, I long to be perfectly whole	134
Did Christ o'er sinners weep?	204
Dear Father, to thy mercy-seat	124
ETERNITY	73
Enthroned is Jesus now	78
Free salvation is flowing	1
From worldly tho't and busy care	2
FOR OTHER FOUNDATION	28
Full of sin though I may be	35
Far from my Father	39
FOR SUCH AS I	45
FULLY PERSUADED	89
FULL SALVATION	91
Forever here my rest shall be	132
Fade, fade each earthly joy	166
From every stormy wind that blows	172
For perhaps the dreaded future	209
GLAD TIDINGS	1
God, the All-wise, beholding sinners	30
GLIDING DOWN LIFE'S RIVER	32
Go to the Savior	52
GATHERING ONE BY ONE	79
GIVE YOURSELF TO JESUS	81
Going; ah, yes, I am going	107
Give me the wings of faith to rise	185
HE'LL RECEIVE YOU	3
How sweet t'will be to find	8
HAIL THE GREAT EMANCIPATION	30
HE CLEANSES ME	50
How my spirit yearns	50
Holy Spirit, hear my cry	67
Hope is singing	87
HE SAVES	101
HE KNOWETH THE WAY I TAKE	102
HAVE YOU NOT A WORD FOR JESUS	104
HOME	107
HO! EVERY ONE	116
He lendeth me	142
Holy Spirit, faithful guide	157
How sweet, how heavenly is the sight	205
IN THE PRAYER-ROOM	3
I am the light	6
I want thy heart	7
IS IT THERE? WRITTEN THERE?	12
I do not ask for the pride of earth	12
I CHOOSE TO FOLLOW JESUS	15
IS THERE ANY ONE HERE	16
IS YOUR LAMP BURNING, BROTHER	23
I have found repose	27
In this world of sin and ruin	32
Is there a sinner awaiting?	36

Title	No.
I am Thine	37
I Heard the Voice of Jesus	40
I've a home over yonder	57
I Know that Jesus Loves Me	68
I know not what shall befall me	64
I'm fully saved thro' Jesus' blood	69
I am waiting, O my Father	76
I have given my all to Jesus	80
I am Sweetly Saved in Jesus	83
I will cling to the cross	84
It is Better Farther on	87
I bring you tidings	88
I'm fully persuaded	89
I have seen a mother weeping	95
In a world so full of weeping	97
In Sight of the Crystal Sea	103
I sat alone with life's memories	103
I shall not want	112
I have heard my Savior calling	114
I gave my life for thee	119
In the Christian's home in glory	141
I stand all bewildered	150
In the cross of Christ I glory	154
In some way or other	155
I am coming to the cross	156
I have a Savior	160
I hear the Savior say	162
I left all with Jesus	165
I love thy kingdom, Lord	176
In the silent midnight watches	183
I saw a wayworn trav'ler	208
Jesus came down	21
Jesus is Passing this Way	36
Jesus Cares for Me	47
Jesus all the Way	55
Jesus My Savior Dear	63
Jesus is pleading	74
Jesus Died for Me	93
Jesus My all	96
Jesus, Meek and Gentle	100
Joy! Joy!	110
Jesus, lover of my soul	118
Jesus is gone up on high	194
Jesus, assembled in thy name	196
Jesus, my Lord	203
Just as I am	206
Knocking, knocking, who is there?	153
Lead Me On	24
Lost in our sins	34
Look Up	38
Lost for Want of a Word	58
Lord Revive Us	85
Lord, at thy mercy-seat	96
Lord, dismiss us	149
More Love to Thee	44
My Anchor is Holding	71
My soul looks in yon paradise	72
My Soul is Singing of Jesus	75
Mighty rock whose towering form	77
Mercy for All	86
My faith looks up to thee	136
My hope is built on nothing less	163
Must Jesus bear the cross alone	192
No love to give	20
Nothing but a Contrite Heart	35
Not Knowing	64
Neglect Him No More	99
Neglect not the grace	99
Nearer, my God, to thee	121
Nothing but leaves	177
Oh, Let Me In	7
O, Prodigal, Don't Stay Away	13
O, builders, haste to the rock	28
Once for All	31
Our High Priest	34
Only in the Name of Jesus	41
Out and Into	42
Out of the distance	42
Oh, hear my cry	51
Oh, I hear a voice within me	54
Only Believe	56
Oh, my Father, wilt thou bless me?	62
Only Remembered by what I Have Done	65
Our Comforter and Guide	67
One by one the bonds are severed	79
Oh, the wondrous love	83
Of all the thoughts	93
Oh, now I see the crimson wave	113
Oh, come to the cross	115
Oh, how sweet are the moments	117
Oh, think of the home over there	129
Oh, happy day	145
Oh, to be nothing, nothing	151
Oh, eyes that are weary	170
One sweetly solemn thought	182
Oh, turn ye	184
Oh, how happy are they	188
O Lord, thy work revive	191
Oh, for a thousand tongues to sing	193
Oh, bliss of the purified	201
Oh, to be ready	202
One there is above all others	207
Poor and needy	47
Precious Savior	91
Precious promise God hath given	131
Repent ye	46
Redeemed	53
Redeemed, oh, wondrous love divine	53
Rejoice, His Name is Jesus	88
Rock of ages	128
Return, O wanderer, return	130
Revive thy work, O Lord	159
Sinner so thoughtless	9
Salvation Full and Free	11
Soft and low the Spirit whispers	22
Say, is your lamp burning?	23

	No.
Sing and Rejoice	60
Sitting at the Feet of Jesus	61
Saved Even Now	69
Sweet hope, the anchor of my soul	71
Shall I Be Saved To-night	74
Satisfied By and By	78
Sowing in the morning	90
So near the door	94
Satisfied	112
Send Me	114
Sweet Moments of Prayer	117
Sowing the seed by the daylight fair	140
Savior, thy dying love	164
Savior, like a shepherd lead us	167
Stand up, stand up for Jesus	168
Simply trusting every day	169
Sweet hour of prayer	197
Sun of my soul	200
Shall we meet beyond the river	137
The Mercy-seat	2
'Tis a blessed place to be	3
The Nearer I Draw to Jesus	4
The Crossing Place	8
The Voice of Mercy	9
To the Savior's waiting arms	14
The Still Small Voice	22
Trav'ling to the better land	24
Trusting in the Promise	27
Thine, Jesus, thine	37
There is peace only in his name	41
Tarry no Longer	52
The Voice of the Spirit	54
'Tis Jesus when the burdened heart	55
The Heavenly Home	57
The Potter and the Clay	59
The Savior made atonement	68
Take Thou My Hand	66
There is a home of beauty	75
There's a Better Time a-Coming	92
'Twas Rum that Spoiled my Boy	95
Trust in Jesus only, ever	101
Thro' the wearisome hours	102
The New Song	105
There are songs of joy	105
Thus God Declares His Sovereign Will	106
The Cleansing Wave, 113. See	113

	No.
The great physician	120
The mistakes of my life	126
To-day the Savior calls	127
There is a fountain filled with blood	138
There were ninety and nine	139
Take my life and let it be	147
Tell me the old, old story	148
The judgment day is coming	174
'Tis midnight, and on Olive's brow	179
The Lord into his garden comes	189
There is life in a look	198
Unto Him That Hath Loved Us	80
Unto Thee Will I Cling	84
Up and away	65
Wonderful Savior	6
Whoever receiveth	10
Waiting for Jesus	17
We are sitting by the wayside	17
When I Walk Through the Valley	18
While Jesus whispers to you	19
We'll Bear the Cross	20
Wilt Thou Receive Me	39
Watchman Tell Us of the Night	43
Who'ld Bear the Gospel Banner	48
Wilt Thou Bless Me	62
We Come a Mighty Legion	70
We have heard the call to rally	70
Waiting for His Coming	72
Waiting for the Light	76
We are bought with a price	86
While the Years are Rolling On	97
When I can read my title clear	133
What a friend we have in Jesus	135
What! lay my sins on Jesus?	143
When thou, my righteous Judge	161
We praise Thee, O God	173
While life prolongs its precious light...... 199. And	175
When my final farewell	180
Watchman, tell me, does the morning	181
We're traveling home to heaven above	195
Ye valiant soldiers of the cross	60

www.ingramcontent.com/pod-product-compliance
Lightning Source LLC
Chambersburg PA
CBHW030344170426
43202CB00010B/1238